POLICING IN A DIVERSE SOCIETY

POLICING IN A DIVERSE SOCIETY

ANOTHER AMERICAN DILEMMA

Mary S. Jackson

EAST CAROLINA UNIVERSITY

CAROLINA ACADEMIC PRESS

Durham, North Carolina

Library of Congress Cataloging-in-Publication Data

Jackson, Mary S.
  Policing in a diverse society : another American dilemma / by Mary S.
Jackson.
     p.   cm.
  Includes index.
  ISBN 1-59460-013-9
1. Police-community relations--United States. 2. Community policing--
United States. 3. Minorities--United States. 4. Multiculturalism--United
States. 5. Culture conflict--United States. 6. Discrimination in law enforce-
ment--United States. I. Title.

  HV7936.P8J33 2004
  363.2'3'080973--dc22

                                                              2004018646

CAROLINA ACADEMIC PRESS
700 Kent Street
Durham, NC 27701
Telephone (919) 489-7486
Fax (919) 493-5668
www.cap-press.com

Printed in the United States of America

Dedicated to the East Carolina University criminal justice students who helped me prepare this textbook; all of us had to overcome our fears of being labeled racist or homophobic in order to participate in class presentations and discussions.

CONTENTS

PREFACE

American-authored texts will often, consciously or unconsciously, reflect American perspectives to the point of using biased language such as racism, majority population, dominant population, ethnic identity, mainstream, and impoverished. Not only is such terminology biased and judgmental, but the propensity of ideas and thoughts initiated by image are based on dominant or majority values. For example, while popular thought has moved away from the melting pot metaphor toward a mosaic, those groups that strive to become pluralistic by clinging to ancestral heritage are often labeled militant, separatist, or un-American. Law enforcement officers and criminal justice students must not only remain abreast of the ever-changing terminology, but must try to understand society's cultural diversity.

This text is not intended to equip students with the skills needed to formulate intervention strategies when working with diverse populations (however strategies may arise indirectly as students become aware of how diverse, and yet how similar, Americans really are). This text is not meant to place blame, formulate a paradigm for practice, or discuss policy implications related to policing in a diverse society. Finally, this text is not meant to be just another piece of incomprehensible scholarly work. The intent of this text is to:

1. Provide students with information about minorities in the hopes that the next generation of law enforcement officers, correctional officers, attorneys, and parole/probation officers will function more effectively in America's diverse society;
2. Raise awareness amongst students and law enforcement officers not only of the existing societal diversity, but of key historical events that have impacted individuals and/or groups;
3. Familiarize students with stereotypes, prejudices, and discrimination that can impact individual and group attitudes and behaviors;
4. Encourage students to develop self-awareness and understand how personal, racial, and ethnic biases can impact decision-making and performance; and

5. Teach students to think about people different from themselves, considering how distinct views might impact their fulfilling their duties as law enforcement officers or agents of the court.

Once criminal justice students are aware of diversity amongst individuals, groups, and historical perspectives, they will likely feel more comfortable discussing strategies for working with these specific populations. Furthermore, students will have a better sense of their own limitations as well as a greater appreciation for diversity, which should enhance job performance.

While this text provides an overview to the many racial and ethnic groups, it is anticipated that students will learn two primary concepts: first, the differences in racial and ethnic backgrounds and American ideologies; and second, how such diversity plays an important role when working with colleagues, suspects, and defendants.

The first two chapters discuss diversity and components involved in community policing, to demonstrate to students and those interested in law enforcement how diversity can impact the performance of their duties. The next nine chapters focus on different minority groups (Native Americans, Asian Americans, African Americans, Hispanics, Elderly, Hate Groups, and Gays and Lesbians) with regard to their interactions with police. Discussion highlights events influential in shaping minority groups' perceptions of and relationships with law enforcement agents. Finally, the last chapter discusses the Crime Bill, Affirmative Action, and future projects.

It is important, when reading, to keep in mind that my overall objective is not to ensure political correctness, but to initiate discussion on relevant issues that can no longer be ignored by criminal justice professionals.

ACKNOWLEDGMENTS

I am deeply indebted to my colleagues who reviewed the chapters—Harvey and Heather Jackson, Brandon Evans, Marshall Page, Byron Mintz, and Robert Judson Price—and my editor, Penny Austen. Without their critical editing, this book would not have been possible.

Special thanks to David, who continues to guide and teach me. His tenacity, industriousness, strength, patience, and insight have made the quality of life better for many adolescents and police officers. Also thanks to Lt. Reggie Wright, Chief Hourie L. Taylor, and the Compton Gang Unit (E. Aguirre, T. Brennan, B. Ladd, and R. Richardson) and Officers J. Jackson, V. Locklin, E. Strong, and Paredes.

And my thanks to the ladies and gentlemen referred to as gang members—without their help, knowledge of this area would be limited.

Policing in a Diverse Society

CHAPTER 1

INTRODUCTION: POLICING IN A DIVERSE SOCIETY

Learning Objectives

1. Explain why law enforcement officers should study diversity.
2. Discuss specific terms relating to diversity.
3. Consider the importance of the Civil Rights Act of 1964.
4. Explain the relationship between policing and diversity.
5. Understand the media's role in policing diverse populations.

Why Should Criminal Justice Students Study Diversity?

Criminal justice students often enter law enforcement for ideological and/or personal reasons. For some, such a career is inter-generational (fathers, mothers, and grandparents were police officers). For others, the profession seems glamorous, they want to "kick butt," or they want to help others. Given the complexities inherent to the career, however, the criminal justice student must understand that there is more to law enforcement than taking an oath and carrying a badge—one must accept the accompanying responsibilities.

Diversity in American society is ever-growing. Throughout their careers, students will interact with racially or ethnically diverse partners and administrators, and will witness discrimination as people exploit and vilify diversity. Students must not only be aware of the diversity, but must try to understand it. Kochman highlights five reasons for criminal justice students to study diversity: Cross Cultural Era, Ethnic Renewal, Hate Crimes, World Events, and Job Safety and Performance (Kochman 1993).

3

Cross Cultural Era

American society is undergoing rapid change. The twenty-first century has seen the Latino population become the number one minority group, growing faster than the entire population (from 35.3 percent of the population in 2000 to 38.8 percent in 2002), with African Americans the second largest (12.9% of the population). The Census Bureau estimates that people of color will eventually comprise the majority of the population, and the aging baby boomer generation will comprise twenty percent (Bernstein & Bergman 2003).

Along with these changing demographics, families are changing. No longer are families defined as a husband and wife (man and woman), two children, and a pet. Today's families include single heads of households or same-sex couples with children. As trans-racial adoptions continue to increase, family members may not even look alike.

There is concern that racial categorizing has been used to define what a family should or should not be. Traditional racial categories are outdated. Children of mixed heritage question why they must choose a single race for classification purposes. In response to pressure by biracial groups and special interest groups, the U.S. Government debated whether the 2000 census should use terms like "biracial" or "multiracial" instead of "other" for those of mixed racial heritage (Daniel 2002). Some see no need for categories. This would, of course, raise a host of other issues. Police officers would have greater difficulty capturing suspects with ambiguous racial identities, and it would be difficult to identify discrimination in the workplace, schools, and housing (Daniel 2002).

Ethnic Renewal

Ethnic renewal implies that people seek an increased understanding of their identity so as to reach their fullest potential. This can occur with any individual or group, and can be positive or negative. For example, during the African American ethnic renewal of the 1960s and 1970s when Stokley Carmichael was expounding black pride, many whites and less-radical blacks became concerned that this thinking was revolutionary and corrosive. As African Americans experienced the fourth major renewal phase during the 1980s and 1990s (the first three being slavery, reconstruction, and the 1960s), many were still searching for their roots.

The ethnic renewal process is not unique to African Americans. Other groups such as Jews, Germans, and Irish, also seek renewal. As immigrants enter the country, they disprove Myrdal's (1944) melting pot hypothesis by proudly transposing their cultures and beliefs on their new environment.

Goode (2001) describes America as a blend of racial and ethnic groups. The theme of the 1980s and 1990s was pluralistic categorization, in which each group struggled to maintain its own identity, resisting assimilation to the point of being undifferentiated from the majority population (Lamphere 2001). Today, America is moving away from the idea of the melting pot toward the mosaic where minority and ethnic populations strive to preserve their heritage and culture.

World Events

Media and technology have made the world a much smaller place. Within seconds, one can see how global problems affect Americans. For example, soldiers are engaged in Bosnia, Iraq, Afghanistan, Korea, Nigeria, and Latin America, all countries with values and communication methods unlike our own (Kochman 1993). It has been said that America offers world policing— a statement that, especially in light of the current Iraq war, conveys America's role as a world power. Since the September 11, 2001 (9/11) attacks on the World Trade Center and the Pentagon, America has led the charge in the war against terrorism by toppling the regimes of Saddam Hussein and the Taliban. Not only do international events impact American society—affirmative action, abortion, trans-racial adoptions, gay marriages, and gays in the military also stimulate debate over discriminatory practices. Americans, therefore, must understand how to communicate with others whose cultures and values differ.

Hate Crimes

Racism still exists in America, in a new, covert form. College students thinking they are pledging a Greek fraternity or sorority, for example, may discover to their horror that they have become recruits of a hate group. Many such groups are composed of paramilitary men and women with some degree of military and/or law enforcement experience. Not only do they commit acts against individuals and groups, but some have joined together against the U.S. Government. The Freedman of Montana, for example, negotiated with government officials for eighty-one days over their surrender from the Montana farmhouse they occupied. The Arizona Viper Militia was discovered testing bombs in the Arizona desert and, according to undercover informants, was plotting to bomb federal buildings.

Steps are being taken to address this new form of racism. President George H. Bush signed the Hate Crime Statistics Act of 1990, a law stipulating that crimes of race, religion, sexual orientation, or ethnicity come under federal jurisdiction (Jenness and Broad 1997). The FBI is investigating the bombings of African American churches. The U.S. Department of Justice disclosed that some of its personnel made a point of making racial slurs at a social function. These people received a letter of warning. One could argue, of course, that what government personnel do on their own time should exist outside government scrutiny.

Job Performance and Safety

Job performance and safety are separate but related issues. Competent officers, for example, are not always safe because they may not understand the need to work in partnership with the diverse community to reduce crime. If the officer understands these things, the community can offer him safety. Some officers feel protected simply because they are wearing a blue uniform—they feel they don't need to understand the community and its diverse population. When under pressure, however, this "Blue Shield" can fall, and the safety net of the "Silent Code" can fail. Further, this attitude can cause performance problems as the community will not assist officers with "attitude problems." These officers may therefore resort to harsh tactics in order to perform their duties. The personnel of a police department should, theoretically, reflect the diverse composition of the community that it serves.

Diversity Terms

Communication is an attempt to interact with others in a verbal or non-verbal manner. It is central in policing to understanding diversity, as a lack of willingness or capability to communicate will likely strain relationships.

Racism, as defined in this text, is the belief that physical appearance (race) accounts for differences in human character or ability. Brown (2001) suggests that every American citizen is at some point exposed to racism. Many are aware of racism, directly or indirectly experiencing its effects, but deny or rationalize its existence. Some take action against it. Others feel unaffected, and therefore see no need to analyze its nature and scope. Many would like to believe that it no longer exists, but as Justice Sandra Day O'Connor stated in *Adarand v. Pena* (1995), racism still exists in American society.

Ethnocentrism refers to the belief in the superiority of an individual's racial and ethnic heritage. The term was first used by William Graham Sumner (Brown 2003). Unlike racism, which has a negative connotation, ethnocentrism can be positive or negative. Positive ethnocentrism is seen when attempting to raise one's self-esteem, strengthen racial and ethnic identity, and instill patriotism. Ethnocentrism becomes negative when used by hate groups to justify unequal treatment or elimination of a racial or ethnic group. Hitler used both racism and ethnocentrism during the 1930s, when he proclaimed the need to eliminate those not possessing Germanic physical characteristics.

The term biracial is used to classify individuals of mixed heritage. Some, however, prefer to be called "multicultural" or "multiethnic." Golfer Tiger Woods, for example, refers to himself as multicultural because of his mixed racial background (black, Portuguese, and Oriental). Recording artist Mariah Carey refers to herself as biracial because her father is African American. Theoretically, but not legally, she has determined her own racial classification.

During the slavery era, the concept of "passing" came into play—some biracial slaves (who might have been considered multicultural in the 1990s) capitalized on their physical characteristics by allowing themselves to be classified as white. Today, social scientists use the term assimilation to refer to an individual's blending into a group—a process that varies in ease and length of time depending on whether physical and cultural differences exist between the ethnic or racial groups (Van den Berghe 1981). There are different types of assimilation: cultural, structural and biological. Cultural assimilation involves the adoption of the dominant group's cultural traits such as language, religion, clothing styles, values, and beliefs (Scupin 2003). Structural assimilation involves becoming a participant in basic institutions, such as neighborhood organizations or churches. Biological assimilation involves procreation, reproduction, or intermarriage between groups.

Assimilation waned in the 1990s. Increasingly, individuals sought identification with and acceptance by both dominant racial and ethnic nomenclatures, resulting in a multicultural or multiethnic classification. Given the diverse nature of American society, however, it is becoming difficult to identify individuals or groups who are not multicultural. By adding a sixth racial category to the census, the U.S. Government has opted to allow citizens to identify themselves. For the first time since the census began in 1790, the 2000 census included a "Two or more races" category. Of the total U.S. population, 6.9 million (2.4 percent) fell into this category (Jones & Smith 2001).

Ethnicity focuses on national origin, religion, and creed, and is based on the idea that a group shares a common history, culture, or ancestry (Scupin 2003). There are two forms of ethnicity: objective and subjective. The objective refers to observable culture and shared symbols such as language, clothing, hairstyles, or religious traditions. The subjective is more intangible: a collective feeling or a desire to display a shared belief (Scupin 2003).

The concept of race is controversial; it is said to be invalid (Montagu 1997) and in need of replacement (MacEachern 2003). Essentially, it is a social construct that represents biogenetic or hereditary factors that distinguish individuals and groups (Anthias 1990).

Race differs from ethnicity in several ways. The biological use of the term implies a certain hereditary composition, while the cultural use arises from an ideological perspective. Personal preference in labeling oneself a member of a racial group, for example, is important (Kennedy 1995; Mays et al. 2003; Brace 2000). Ethnicity, however, ignores physical considerations. It comes from the Greek term "ethnos" (used to refer to non-Greeks), meaning the individual's culture or background, values, and beliefs.

Culture, an acquired schema that includes knowledge, belief, morals, law, and customs, is important to consider when discussing diversity because it is central to explaining human behavior. Culture includes components such as weapons, politics, and all aspects of human activity (Scupin 2003).

Prejudice and discrimination are terms often inappropriately assumed interchangeable. Prejudice is a preconceived thought or attitude, formed without substantiating factual evidence and often based on stereotypical conceptualizations. Discrimination goes beyond racist attitudes and beliefs by targeting individuals and/or groups with policies, procedures, and laws (Long 1997). Discriminatory actions exclude individuals and groups based on race, ethnicity, gender, sexual orientation, or religion. Discrimination is easier to combat than prejudicial thinking, because it is illegal. Until now, the most salient weapon against institutionalized discrimination has been the Civil Rights Act of 1964. This act, amended in 1968, 1972, and 1990, prohibits discrimination in education, housing, and employment based on race, gender, age, sexual orientation, religion, or ethnicity.

Stereotypes are those expectations derived from myths about individuals or groups. Stereotyping is a method of assigning individual attributes to groups (Long 1997). The term was first used in 1922 by Walter Lippmann, who suggested that stereotypes are mental pictures that emerge because of lack of personal experience (Marger 1994). Such pictures are usually so firmly entrenched in the preconscious mind that stereotypical thinking about individuals and groups becomes reality.

Stereotypes have been supported by scientific racialism (Lieberman 2003). Todorov (1993) explained the difference between racialism and racism: racialism is an ideology or doctrine, whereas racism is a practice of discriminating against individuals perceived to be inferior (Lieberman 2003). Whether an ideology or a practice, individuals make decisions about others based on race. Of major importance is the individual's worldview—his definition of reality that serves as the foundation for his attitudes and beliefs.

Diversity denotes differences. Discussions of cultural diversity or multiculturalism are often limited to black/white issues. Police officers, however, are faced with far more complex challenges. The U.S. Constitution provides safeguards to individuals and groups, ensuring that officers "serve and protect" all citizens—not just those who look and talk like them.

It is important to consider not only issues in diversity, but how different groups have contributed to shaping and strengthening American society. Often the media, that Foley and Moss (2001) consider a critical agent in the American socialization process (a primary means of explaining societal events), negatively depicts police and diversity in terms of black/white issues. Police officers are often portrayed as unaware villains and, when faced with a situation requiring knowledge of diversity, are often left feeling embarrassed, ignorant, or scared. These fears are stimulated by the known (criminal behavior) as well as the unknown or unconscious (stereotyping). Many police organizations require that their officers undergo diversity/multicultural training, however these sessions are too few, too limited in scope (e.g., only discussions of black/white), and superficial.

Summary

Criminal justice students must study issues of diversity to understand the changing demographics and composition of families in today's cross cultural era, the impact of ethnic renewals and world events, the continued prevalence of hate crimes, and to ensure job safety. The study of diversity, however, presents a dilemma—while it is necessary to understand and interact with individuals and groups in the community, discussing such issues can cause discomfort (many do not want to be labeled by their classmates or instructor) or defensiveness. The classroom, however, offers an environment in which a student can espouse or develop thoughts. Terms are defined to ensure common understanding and enable students to feel at ease using more pejorative ("street") terminology.

Because society is so diverse, it makes sense to learn about its many groups. Fear of the unknown (about individuals or groups) causes errors, unsafe practices, and poor decisions. Without interaction and/or understanding, people tend to perceive other individuals or groups as being one way when in fact they may be totally different. The criminal justice student is entering a field that will require much interaction with diverse populations; it is extremely important to treat everyone with respect and dignity, understand personal biases, and not allow those biases to impact decision-making.

The war with Iraq has prompted many questions. One effective method for answering questions and resolving problems is to gain a better understanding of the topic. For criminal justice students, the study of diversity is a good start.

Key Concepts

Civil Rights Act	Melting Pot
Communication	Mosaic
Discrimination	Passing
Diversity	Prejudice
Ethnicity	Race
Ethnocentrism	Racism

Questions for Discussion

1. Discuss a situation in which you experienced a negative reaction to diversity. How did you react? How did it impact your thinking?
2. Talk with someone else who may have experienced a negative reaction. How does their situation differ from yours? How is it similar?
3. Explain how ethnocentrism differs from racism. Provide examples.
4. Explain why diversity in America involves more than racial issues.
5. As a police officer, how would you handle being teamed up with a "seasoned" officer who makes racial slurs or degrades gays and lesbians?

Suggested Reading

<www.consejo.org/publications.html>. A publication by the Council of Latino Agencies explains the procedures and problems of policing the Latino community in the District of Columbia.

<www.crr.ca/en/MediaCentre/FactSheets/FactAboutPolicing.pdf>. This paper discusses policing in a diverse society and the consequences of racism.

<www.findarticles.com/p/articles/mi_m2194/is_n6_v63/ai_15704715>. This website talks about policing an increasingly diverse America and the cultural aspect that has directed the nation away from the "melting pot."

CHAPTER 2

COMMUNITY POLICING: AN OLD PHILOSOPHY THAT HAUNTS US

Learning Objectives

1. List the advantages and disadvantages of community policing.
2. Compare and contrast community policing with police community relations.
3. Discuss three styles of policing and provide examples of each.
4. Explain the early role of police officers. How is this role viewed by many officers today?
5. Explain the early role of women in law enforcement.

Community Policing vs. Police Community Relations

Police Community Relations (PCR) and community policing are two philosophies aimed at bridging the gap between law enforcement organizations and the community. The aim of PCR is to enhance the community's perception of the police (Adler 1996). PCR, initially designed to improve relations between police and citizens, has responded to social disorder and community unrest (Hess & Wrobleski 1993, 424). Many police departments have implemented initiatives to improve their image—they host town hall meetings to discuss policing styles and community needs, sit on community boards, recruit criminal justice students, allow citizens to "ride along" with officers, and have hired community relations specialists. Critics, however, question the effectiveness of PCR unit officers, and many PCR programs have been abandoned (Walker & Katz 2002).

Community policing differs from PCR as it is an ongoing face-to-face interaction that proactively emphasizes law enforcement partnership with the community for the sake of crime reduction (Haberfeld 2002). A major component is problem solving, or problem-oriented policing, where officers and community residents together identify, assess, and respond to situations (Goldstein 1990).

Although some consider them the same, community policing differs from PCR (Cox & Fitzgerald 1996). According to Taylor et al. (1984), the notion of PCR originated in 1955 at Michigan State University in response to the conflict surrounding the police and minority groups. The first police organization to address this issue was a special community relations division in St. Louis, Missouri, in 1957 (Taylor et al. 1984). PCR, it was assumed, would make citizens more aware of police operations and involve them in crime prevention efforts, thereby easing the tension between the police and community.

A number of researchers (Cox & Fitzgerald 1996; Haberfeld 2002; Senna & Siegel 2001) outlined the major differences between the philosophies (see Table 2.1):

Evolution of American Policing

Researchers have argued that respecting cultural values and beliefs is important in establishing positive community-police relationships. Leinen (1984, 160) argues that continual contact provides the foundation for the relationship. Community policing requires that officers invest in the community, collaborating with citizens to determine the best crime prevention methods (Cox & Fitzgerald 1996; Miller & Hess 1994; Adler et al. 1996). One example of community policing is decentralization, a method illustrated by the Greenville Police Department in North Carolina where officers work out of a community center and interact daily with citizens. For their part, residents (including churches) volunteer time to work with the officers.

Organized American policing first began to control riotous situations in cities such as Boston, Philadelphia, and New York. In 1845, New York became the first American city to have paid police officers (Langworthy & Travis 1994). New York stockbrokers went to England and returned with a model for policing derived from the London Metropolitan Police Act of 1829. This act, originated by Sir Robert Peel, provided for the organization of police activities in

Table 2.1

Community Policing	Police Community Relations
Goal to solve problems	Goal to change attitudes
Line officers regularly contact citizens	Staff officers rarely contact citizens
Citizens identify problems	Blue ribbon committees identify problems
Police are accountable to citizens	Police are accountable to civilian review boards and police supervisors
Real organizational change occurs (selection, training, evaluation)	Organization does not change, some new programs are added
Requires department-wide acceptance of philosophy	Isolated acceptance, often only in PCR unit
Influence is from bottom up (including other citizens)	Influence is from top down, experts make decisions
Officers are always accessible in decentralized locations	Intermittent contact through central headquarters
Officers encourage citizen participation in problem-solving	Citizens encouraged to volunteer, but also to request more services
Success determined by improved quality of life	Success determined by lowered crime rates

a professional, non-hostile manner. Initially, American police officers partially followed the same Peelian principles as the English Bobbies—they remained professional at all times, did not carry guns, and were expected to interact with community residents.

Historically, police officers have functioned much like social workers in that they have had to interact with a diverse community to provide services and aid in problem solving. Wilson (1968) identifies three policing styles: watchman, legalistic, and service. The watchman style is more of an individual approach, in which officers make decisions based on their value system, knowledge base, and best judgment. The legalistic style is grounded in the premise that the law takes precedence over all actions. Even when an officer feels that a situation requires a less stringent response, he must make the decision based solely on the law. The service style, a formal yet more relaxed approach, encompasses the previous two styles; its primary goal is to both provide assistance to and protect individuals, with service ranging from directing traffic to consoling rape victims. In each style, success depends on the officer's ability to intervene effectively in the community.

Strategies

Roberg & Kuykendall (1990) discuss how Wilson's policing styles can be incorporated into the community policing model. Four strategies that might prove effective are: visibility, apprehension, counseling, and education.

1. Visibility involves instilling a sense of safety in the citizenry by observing police officers at work. This can break down stereotypes, such as how officers waste time in doughnut shops, speed through traffic to "get lunch," are rude or corrupt, abuse discretionary powers, follow a code of silence more important than the law, or are "super cops" not fearful of anything. Greater community visibility enables citizens to see, if they choose, what is involved in an officer's eight hour day.

2. Apprehension falls in the crime control category of policing. Because there is a constant cry by politicians to get tough on crime, citizens have become convinced that the only way to reduce crime is to imprison criminals for long periods of time. The crime control model (originally discussed by Herbert Packer), stresses the presumption of guilt and high arrest rates. Thus, many citizens feel that apprehension rates are good indicators that police officers are performing. On the other hand, there are more arrests of minorities than the majority population, suggesting that officers arrest or detain individuals based on race.

3. Counseling is an uncomfortable area for some novice police officers. Historically, before the need existed to carry guns or use force, police officers acted as mentor and counselor to citizens. Many of today's officers have received training to sharpen their counseling skills ("interpersonal skills"). Resource and Drug Awareness Resistance Education (DARE) officers who are placed primarily in schools need such skills, as their main goal is not to arrest students, but to prevent harmful acts and promote conflict resolution.

4. Education is the PCR component of community policing. Police organizations use education to keep the public abreast of their activities and communicate their needs. To understand the community and allow residents to better appreciate what a police officer's job entails, officers are increasingly appearing at town and council gatherings, and meeting with individuals, groups, and organizations. Chief Willie Williams of the Los Angeles Police Department considers community education an important strategy—after a series of riots, he went door to door. The DARE program, while receiving criticism, demonstrates efforts by police organizations to make children and parents more aware of the dangers of drugs.

Effective police intervention, especially using a community policing model, relies on the officer's ability to communicate with citizens. Unlike in the 1920s, 1930s, and even 1940s, immigration has brought increased diversity to society. This raises new challenges for police officers (Shusta et al. 1995) in communication, using discretionary power, the changing composition of police organizations, and the use of alternative strategies.

Communication

Communication is both a verbal and nonverbal process. Communication patterns used by police officers are greatly influenced by education, personal experiences, attitudes, goals, and objectives. Just as social work and psychology students are taught the importance of understanding the "self" before entering their respective professions, police officers should seek this inner knowledge. Unfortunately, many criminal justice programs and police academies fail to emphasize the need for aspiring officers to discover their own worldviews—ironically, the very ideas that will impact how they interact with others and how others will, in turn, interact with them (Roberg & Kuykendall 1990).

Police officers are taught to discriminate during academy training. For example, they are commonly taught that suspects are dangerous and should be incarcerated to protect society. Further, they are taught to identify suspects based on appearance—the guilty suspect is depicted as disheveled and mean-looking, while an innocent bystander is depicted wearing a suit or holding a baby. This thinking is fine so long as it does not become discriminatory by extending stereotypes of racial and ethnic groups.

Mann (1993) suggests that criminal justice professionals make certain assumptions about the criminal tendencies of segments in the population. According to Tonry (1995), affluent or middle class African Americans have been stopped by police simply for seeming "out of place." African American Harvard professor Cornell West, for example, was stopped and falsely accused of cocaine charges. The "out of place" theory is often used for all population segments—officers, for example, monitor whites in drug- infested neighborhoods, assuming that because they live elsewhere, they must be in the area for criminal purposes (Walker & Katz 2002). Many officers, believing all defendants guilty, subconsciously transfer these thoughts into body language (Wallace 1998). The suspect, feeling threatened, may then become uneasy. It is important to be aware that this type of communication may be occurring.

How police officers communicate depends on primary and secondary dimensions of communicating (Kochman 1993). The initial or primary dimension involves placing value on factors such as age, gender, and race. The secondary dimension involves deciding whether the interaction should continue, and the direction it should take (how the person will be treated). This dimension is based on marital status, education, socioeconomic status, religion, military status, and geographical proximity.

Because communication is considered vital to an improved understanding of diversity, one must also consider hindrances to the exchange of ideas. Barriers include prejudices, stereotyping (lending credence to myths regarding all members of a racial or ethnic group), and poor listening skills (only hearing what he/she expects, and no exploration of alternative solutions).

Police officers and criminal justice students should strive to overcome these barriers by improving listening skills, considering the law over personal feelings, and striving to understand racially and ethnically diverse people. Officers take an oath to serve and protect citizens—an oath that is non-discriminatory and all-inclusive.

Discretionary Power

Effective communication between police and citizens is also important because officers have discretionary power to make decisions without supervisory input—decisions influenced not only by training, but by the officers' cultural and personal experiences. This inverted pyramid managerial style is considered effective because officers often do not have time to report to a supervisor when immediate action is needed.

Discretionary power, however, can be abused whenever negative prejudicial attitudes, brutality, and discriminatory practices come to play. Walker (1981) suggests that this power, and the resulting autonomous behavior, has contributed to incidents of police brutality. Klockars (1985) discusses the thin line between legal and illegal police behavior, arguing that the life-or-death decisions being made outweigh the means used to make the decisions. While citizens will tolerate certain "minor" discriminatory practices, they may escalate the importance of such incidents if officers are seen to be selectively enforcing laws.

Selective law enforcement occurs when officers deviate from prescribed legal sanctions and implement their own prescriptions based on the nature of the crime, the circumstances, the perpetrator, and the amount of available evidence. Examples include an officer issuing a verbal warning rather than a written citation for a traffic violation or a domestic violence situation in which the officer decides, contrary to procedure, that a cooling-off period is remedy enough. In all cases, selective law enforcement allows for discrimination by police officers.

Even more police discretion will be used in the proactive community policing model. The inverted pyramid method of administering justice will become more necessary because diverse racial and ethnic groups respond differently to police intervention, and officers will need the latitude to make on-the-spot decisions.

Changing Composition of Police Organizations

As the organizational environment changes and diversifies, police organizations will be increasingly pressured to ensure that their units reflect the community that they serve. Many are recruiting women, people of color, and different ethnic groups. Still, some feel that not enough strides have been made. Others, while admitting that what changes have occurred are beneficial, note that minorities and women must still contend with racism and discrimination. Senna and Siegel (2001) discuss the continuous sexual harassment and discrimination on the police force, while Sowell (2002) cites the limited administrative positions available. It is still not fashionable to hire gay or lesbian persons, and few, if any, departments promote such police officers into administrative positions.

Further, while Hispanic officers in large cities increased from nine percent in 1990 to fourteen percent in 2000, more Spanish-speaking officers need to be hired (Daniels 2002) so as to ensure constitutional safeguards for this minority. An officer's first duty after an arrest is to "Mirandize" the suspect, meaning to. According to the U.S. Supreme Court in *Miranda v. Arizona* (1966), an officer must "Mirandize" (read the individual his rights) a suspect upon arrest. Miranda cards should be available in Spanish so that Spanish-speaking suspects aren't made to wait while a translator is located. An example of a Spanish Miranda warning card (Hess & Wrobleski 1993) is shown in Table 2.2.

The 9/11 terrorist attacks resulted in a renewed focus on Miranda rights, as many arrested were called "enemy combatants" and were denied access to

Table 2.2

Spanish Translation	English Version
Antes que le hagamos cualquier Pregunta, usted tiene que comprender sus derechos.	Before we ask you any questions, you have to understand your rights.
Usted tiene el derecho de guarder silencio.	You have the right to remain silent.
Lo que diga puede usarse contra usted en la corte.	Anything you say can be held against you in a court of law.
Usted tiene el derecho de hablar con un abogado y de tenerio presente con usted mientras le hacemos preguntas.	You have the right to talk to a lawyer and have him/her present with you while you are being questioned.
Si usted no tiene medios para contratar un abogado, La corte le asignara uno antes que le hagamos preguntas, si asi lo desea.	If you can not afford to hire a lawyer, one will be appointed to represent you before any questioning, if you wish.
Usted puede optar en cualquier moment a emplear estos derechos, y asi negarse a Contestar preguntas o hacer declaraciones.	You can decide at any time to exercise these rights, and not answer any questions nor make any statements.
?comprende usted lo que acabo de leerie?	Do you understand what I have just read to you?

attorneys (Cole & Smith 2005). The U.S. Supreme Court revisited the *Miranda* decision in 2000, endorsing it in *Dickerson v. U.S.* (2000) (Cole & Smith 2005). *Miranda* critics claim that reading an individual his rights can cause a delay in obtaining information crucial to homeland security. To be sure, officers working the 9/11 attacks found the Miranda ruling a hindrance. Human rights advocates such as the American Civil Liberties Union (ACLU), on the other hand, cite the need to apply constitutional safeguards and human rights whenever applicable.

It is important that officers have resources (e.g., interpreters) available in times of crisis. The days are long gone when officers could simply kick down doors and make arrests. Officers today must be able to think critically, and understand the people they must serve and protect. To this end, many police departments are requiring college degrees for front line officers.

A second area of change is the educational requirements for entry-level police officers. Sherman (1978) is a strong advocate for educating and training police officers. Such training, however, must include discussions about racial and ethnic group issues. Walker & Katz (2002) suggest that most classroom training has not changed since the 1960s, and there is a need to consider the links between race relations training and improved police behavior and attitudes. More local police departments are recruiting officers with college degrees (e.g., criminal justice, computer sciences) (Hoffman 2000). Many seasoned police officers are returning to school seeking advanced degrees. One can speculate that college degrees provide police officers with problem-solving alternatives other than guns—they are expected to act professionally, be knowledgeable of other cultures, and use common sense.

Birzer & Tannehill (2001) suggest that as changes occur in policing, there is a need to change the way officers are trained. In response to violent criminal acts, the federal police core emerged from the Violent Crime Control & Law Enforcement Act of 1994. Federal funds would be used not only for recruitment, but to train and educate qualified police officers who could work to reduce the crime rate in "challenging communities" (Office of the Police Corps and Law Enforcement Education 2000, 1). Since 1996 when the Police Corps program began in six pilot states (Arkansas, Maryland, Nevada, North Carolina, Oregon, and South Carolina), over twenty-eight states now participate. Each state is responsible for designing curricula that focuses on physical fitness, morality, ethics, character, analytical capabilities, and issues of diversity (Office of Police Corps and Law Enforcement Education 2001, 3).

A third area of change involves the use of video equipment in patrol cars. Eventually, police officers will all use video cameras while patrolling in a car, on foot, or on a bike. As of yet, officers have not fully understood the crime-solving implications of videotaping—the technology has been used more to provide evidence of an officer's innocence as well as guilt. Walker (1977) discusses how brutality and corruption are inherent to the policing profession. While only a small percent of police officers abuse their power, the public will view many as guilty. In the 1990s, three incidents were videotaped in which police officers demonstrated unnecessary cruelty—the 1991 Rodney King incident in which videotape showed white police officers brutally beating an African American male lying on the ground, the 1996 Los Angeles incident in which a helicopter news camera taped officers chasing and beating illegal Mexicans, and the 1996 South Carolina incident in which an officer chased an

African American female, approached her car with gun drawn, and pulled her to the ground. Although the officer later apologized to the woman on national television, the video camera in his car exposed the incident to millions of viewers.

Finally, police organizations have become concerned with the Furhman syndrome, where officers publicly display their contempt for racial and ethnic groups. Critics of *People v. Simpson* (1995) believe that the prosecution lost partly because they failed to thoroughly interview Detective Mark Furhman, lead detective in the investigation, who had been known to have used a number of racial slurs. The defense used this information to plant doubt in the jury's mind about Furhman's credibility. The Los Angeles Police Department and prosecutor are now trying to demonstrate to police officers how personal bias can be used to assist defendants and hinder an investigation.

Women in Policing

Policewomen are emerging as a group to be reckoned with. Initially, women worked in police organizations as civilians. In 1905, women were appointed "safety officers" in Portland, Oregon, to protect women and children primarily from miners and lumberjacks (Myers 1995). Lola Baldwin, the first woman allowed to hold police powers (Roberg & Kuykendall 1993), was not sworn in on regular duty (Martin 1989), however she carried a badge and could make arrests. She remained active in law enforcement until her death in 1957 (Myers 1995). Five years later, on September 12, 1910, Alice Stebbins-Wells was sworn into the Los Angeles Police Department. Like Baldwin, Stebbins-Wells' assignments dealt primarily with women and children, but she received full police powers. She worked endlessly to recruit more women into the profession by touring cities and encouraging the appointment of female police officers. In addition, she founded the International Association of Women Police that provides a basis for the exchange of ideas and support. By 1916, policewomen were no longer a rarity in law enforcement.

As women continue to enter law enforcement, stereotypes (women are weak, emotional, afraid to use weapons, and in need of protection) are slowly being eroded. As male and female police officers increasingly work together, they are discovering that women are competent in filling historically male-dominated roles. There remain, however, too few women in supervisory and administrative positions. According to the International Association of Chiefs of Police (IACP), there are only 123 female chiefs out of seventeen thousand police organizations (IACP 1998, 5).

Women still experience sexual harassment. Senna and Siegel (2001) note how many women in law enforcement are faced with sexual harassment not only from colleagues, but from administrators as well. Women police officers face locker room jokes, treatment as sex objects, ongoing testing of their skills, and the paternalistic belief that they need assistance in the field. The attitude that policing was "men's work" has changed because of the many anti-discrimination laws (Walker & Katz 2002, 107), including:

- Equal Pay Act 1963
- The Civil Rights Act 1964
- Presidential Executive Order 11246
- Age Discrimination Act 1969
- Title XI of the Education Amendment of 1972
- 1972 amendments to Title VII of Civil Rights Act of 1964
- Section 504 of the Rehabilitation Act 1973
- The American With Disabilities Act 1990

Women officers, like their minority male counterparts, also experience stereotypical abuse from citizens. Many community residents, feeling that a woman's place is in the home, are quick to label female officers as uncooperative, cold-blooded, dykes, or bitches (Senna and Siegel 2001). Most citizens, however, have a positive view of female officers (Worden 1993). Indeed, female officers have been able to diffuse volatile situations by presenting themselves in a less forceful manner than their male partners, an approach especially useful in domestic violence situations (Prussel & Lonsway 2001).

The increased presence of females in law enforcement seems to be sensitizing their male colleagues both to their own needs as well as those of citizens in handling situations. Their "car talk" with female partners can be viewed as therapeutic or stress-reducing. More research is needed to determine whether those officers with female partners are indeed psychologically stronger than those with male partners.

Many male officers feel that female officers are not physically strong enough to subdue criminals—antiquated thinking given that the majority of police work is investigation and written reports. According to Senna and Siegel (2001), while physical stamina may be an advantage, it has not been a major factor in police work. Sherman's (1975) work further reveals that women police officers are equally as competent in most areas as their male counterparts. More and more, female officers are disproving the thinking that football, war, and police work are for men only (Senna and Siegel 2001).

African Americans in Policing

There have been efforts to recruit, hire, and train more minority police officers to make law enforcement organizations more representative of society (Martin 1991). Today, African Americans hold more positions in law enforcement than do other minorities (Reaves & Hickman 2002)—for this reason, and given the limited information available on other minorities, African Americans will be the focus of this discussion.

African American policing has been traced as far back as 1805, when the first African American police officers were hired in New Orleans to help capture runaway slaves (Dulaney 1996). Early slave patrol units worked in cooperation with paramilitary, anti-black organizations such as the Ku Klux Klan (KKK). In 1814, free men of color Charles Allegre and Constant Michel served on the New Orleans City Guard. By 1830, however, there were no longer any African Americans on the police force—city managers were ordered to hire all whites. During the 1870s, African Americans reemerged in law enforcement. It was only in the 1960s, however, that African American police officers were really able to advance, when the restrictions to only policing African American communities were lifted (Senna and Siegel 2001). Prior to this point, African American officers were involved in a cultural matching process; they policed African American communities, often on foot, working alone or with other African American officers.

Although African American officers still face discrimination, they have proven equally as competent as their white counterparts. Two concerns consistently emerge when discussing African American police officers. Some militant whites believe that there are too many minorities on the force—a concern that has developed as police departments aggressively recruit more minorities. Many white men attribute this move to affirmative action (see chapter 12); police departments, however, claim they need more officers aware of, and able to interact with, different cultures. Walker & Katz (2002) discuss how, as city populations have changed, so too have police forces—in Detroit, for example, three-quarters of the population is African American, as is sixty-three percent of the police force.

The second concern is double marginality, a term coined by Nicholas Alex (1969) implying that African American police officers (foot patrol officers and administrators) struggle emotionally with their roles when, in the community, they are classified as "the man" while at the same time facing pressures to join the movement against "the man" (Roberg & KuyKendall 1993; Radelet 1986; Alex 1969). These officers, to prove their loyalty to the blue, treat other minorities harsher than they would non-minorities—they are, therefore, considered sell outs by the minority community, and yet are still not fully accepted by their white counterparts. In the 1800s, slave patrols were used to track down, punish, and control slaves (Haberfeld 2002); in the 1940s and 1950s, African American officers were made to guard businesses they couldn't patronize, and witnessed their fellow white police officers harass, shoot, and kill other African Americans.

The emotional strain caused by double marginality has led to the formation of many African American police organizations (e.g., Afro American Patrolman's League, Black Fraternal Order of Police, Black Shields, NOBLE, and the National Black Police Officers Association). These organizations not only provide emotional support, but also act as a catalyst for bringing about change in policies, hiring practices, departmental racism, and greater access to promotions (Leinen 1984, 27).

The term double marginality also applies as the African American community struggles with the need to have a representative police force while simultaneously distrusting officers who have traditionally symbolized brutality and oppression. The black community, while thankful for African American police officers, remain suspicious knowing that they 1) must perform twice as well as their white counterparts, 2) must constantly demonstrate their loyalty to blue by using stringent tactics in dealing with minorities, and 3) must withstand the notion that they have sold out the African American community. Still, because the community takes care of its own, African American police officers are still able to gain access to information closed off to many white officers.

The majority of interactions between citizens and police officers (regardless of race or ethnicity) are civil—only about five percent are hostile (Walker & Katz 2002). Most citizens appreciate police intervening to maintain law and order, just as most officers want to work well with citizens (Cole & Smith 2005).

Community policing, in promoting positive interactions, seems to help dispel myths held by both police officers and citizens. While not the panacea, community policing is a start in the right direction toward establishing a society in which citizens and police officers work proactively in partnership to reduce crime.

Summary

Community policing, while practiced since the inception of modern policing, has created dilemmas for both police officers and community residents. Residents, regardless of their racial, ethnic, religious, or sexual orientation, depend on the police to enforce laws and maintain order. Of concern, however, is whether officers discriminate while performing their duties. Officers, on the other hand, feel empowered to enforce laws as they deem necessary, and claim that the job requires a certain amount of discrimination.

While every police department in America abides by the slogan "to serve and protect," this poses a real dilemma for law enforcement officers. Like social workers, police officers are sworn to protect and serve society; unlike social workers, however, officers are granted extended powers of discretion in using weapons and/or deadly force. This discretion, or "selective law enforcement," can be viewed as a necessary evil, especially if used as a vehicle to discriminate. Officers can use discretion to determine whether a crime has been committed and what, if any, action will be taken. Some officers discriminate against individuals or groups because of the selective discretionary powers and the limited monitoring by law enforcement administrators.

One method used to monitor this power is the use of civilian review boards. These boards, usually composed of neighborhood residents, evaluate and provide suggestions to local police units, and hear citizen complaints. Members, however, are usually appointed by a city official, whose goal is to make the police department look favorable; while police administrators may feel that civilian review boards are theoretically sound, in practice they are not needed (Miller & Hess 1994).

Police officers were first to the scene when the North Tower of the World Trade Center collapsed, maintaining order in a time of distress. The over seven hundred thousand police officers in America are expected to be in the forefront of decision-making and problem-solving when it comes to crime reduction (Cole & Smith 2005). The use of discretion is not only an expectation, but a requirement.

The twenty-first century has brought changes that have and will continue to impact policing. For example, policing has traditionally been characterized as a paramilitary organization composed primarily of white males who adhered to an internal code of silence, or a "Blue Code." Acts involving discretion, while possibly unconstitutional, were seldom the focus of attention. Because of the *Simpson* trial, police departments nationwide no longer tolerate questionable actions and racial discrimination by officers. Today, officers are expected to investigate a crime scene and interview witnesses in a professional and non-reproachable manner, regardless of the racial, ethnic, religious, or socio-economic status of those involved. This poses dilemmas for officers in three areas:

1. Laws. Officers must understand the law in order to enforce it. Laws, however, are ambiguous, varying between states and ever-changing. Many laws, existing for centuries without revision, are left up to the discretion of the enforcer.
2. Efficacy of the political arena. The political climate impacts how policing is incorporated into Wilson's various policing styles. For example,

there is currently debate over the issue of community policing or problem solving oriented policing, both service style approaches. Legislators support community policing and, as a sign of confidence, have appropriated billions of dollars in the form of a crime bill to implement the strategy.

3. Changing demographics in society. Changing demographics have made it necessary for police departments to become more aggressive in recruiting women and minorities in order to ensure that police officers are truly representative of society. Communities also want ongoing training of police officers in cultural competency.

Communities benefit from the watchman style of policing in which officers provide assistance in a public relations manner. The legalistic (professional) style stresses the enforcement aspects of policing; police officers are well-trained and efficient. While the legalistic style is more objective, it is also the most forceful; because some minorities and special interest groups have claimed that this style focuses primarily on arrest rates and brutality, the officer's role as crime fighter is closely scrutinized. The service style depicts the police officer as a collaborative partner, seeking to work together with citizens to prevent crime. Today, this style is receiving the most attention. Regardless of which policing style is used, officers must be cognizant of their personal biases, act professionally, understand and communicate effectively with diverse populations, and use sound judgment.

Although, police departments today are comprised of more minorities and women on the front line than in the twentieth century, recruitment needs to target even more female administrators and Hispanic officers. In light of the fight against terrorism and the increase in diverse communities, officers must be well-trained and able to think critically (especially in times of crisis) at the local, national, and international levels.

Key Concepts

Alice Stebbins-Wells	Police Community Relations
Barriers to communication	Police discretion
Community policing	Primary dimension
Double Marginality	Relations
Furhman Syndrome	Secondary dimension
Lola Baldwin	Selective law enforcement
NOBLE enforcement	Styles of policing

Questions for Discussion

1. Explain police discretion and provide examples. Discuss pros and cons.
2. What impact might the Furhman syndrome have on policing? Provide examples (real or hypothetical).
3. Communication is extremely important when interacting with citizens. Discuss barriers that can hinder communication between police officers and citizens. Explain how the barriers can be reduced or eliminated.
4. The media plays a major role in perceptions. How have television and movies impacted the image of policing in American society?
5. What are some obstacles that females face as law enforcement officers? Discuss how sexual harassment can be dealt with in police organizations.

Suggested Reading

Dulaney, W. 1996. *Black Police in America.* Bloomington, IN: Indiana University Press.

Senna, J. & Siegel, L.J. 2001. *Essentials of Criminal Justice.* Belmont, CA: Hoover Institute Press.

Sowell, T. 2002. *Beyond the Color Line: Discriminating, Economics, and Culture.* Boston, MA: Allyn and Bacon.

Wallace, H. 1998. *Victimology: Legal, Psychological, and Social Perspectives.* Boston, MA. Allyn and Bacon.

<www.cicp.org>. The Carolina Institute for Community Policing home page—provides an overview of community policing, and a list of further readings and web sources.

<http://cj.wadsworth.com/cole_smithcia4e>. Cole & Smith on how racial bias affects police decisions.

<www.met.police.uk/history>. Cole & Smith (2005) discuss the history of London's Metropolitan Police.

<www.ncjrs.org/policing/fem635.htm>. Cole & Smith provide more information on the history of women in policing.

<www.policing.com>. Website designed to provide the latest information, training, advice, and discussion on community policing.

CHAPTER 3

NATIVE AMERICANS AND POLICING

Learning Objectives

1. Explain the significance of the Dawes Act of 1887.
2. Identify the significance of the Indian Removal Act of 1830.
3. Discuss the significance of the Certificates of Degree of Indian Blood (CDIB).
4. Discuss the Trail of Tears and its significance to Native American history.
5. Discuss policing issues on and off reservations.

Historical Perspective

When and how Native Americans came to North America is a matter for debate. Thornton (1987) provides both Euro and Native American explanations regarding their origins. From the Euro-religious perspective, all humans descended from Adam and Eve. From the Native American perspective, the emphasis is on earth as the creator. The Zuni, Creek, and Kiowa tribes, for example, believe that they were created by the earth (Thornton 1987). Whatever their origins, history validates that Native Americans inhabited North America long before Christopher Columbus' 1492 arrival at what he thought was the East Indies (Bonney 2003).

Native Americans were besieged by three conquering nations: the French who came seeking commerce in fur trading, the Spanish seeking gold, and the British hoping to establish settlements (Bonney 2003). As researchers reviewed Columbus' notes, they found that he had not discovered America, but rather had encountered a different race of people in the Bahamas. Both Columbus and Amerigo Vespucci (credited with discovering North America) negatively characterized the natives in fatalistic stereotypical terms (Sauer 1971). The actions and behaviors that they described, however, were quite the opposite—how Native Americans welcomed the strangers with childlike naivety, provided them with food and women, treated them with dignity, and showed them how to survive (Morison 1974, 66). Surely, these traits are not characteristic of "savages" (Sider 1987). There remains debate over an agreed-upon definition of "Indians," as neither the federal government, Congress, nor the courts have provided a uniform, legal definition (Bonney 2003).

Decline of Native Americans

Early Europeans and Euro-Americans called the Native Americans "Indians" or "Los Indios," meaning people of a darker race (Sider 1987). This marked the beginning of racial discrimination (a power stratification system based primarily on physical characteristics), and the decline and annihilation of the Native American race (genocide) (Sider 1987). Factors that have led to their demise include: enslavement, separation, wars, discrimination, lack of adequate food supplies, and the introduction of alcoholism.

Enslavement

Many Indians were captured, tortured, and forced to build living quarters for the Spaniards, provide for their daily needs, perform household chores, and care for the children. Accustomed to living in harmony with the land and worshiping as they pleased, Indians showed the same psychological stress as is evident among most oppressed groups—depression, exposure to contagious diseases (e.g., measles, chicken pox, tuberculosis, and smallpox), and feelings of hopelessness.

Separation

Native Americans experienced two major separations. First, Spaniards forced some (those they considered the best to exhibit) to accompany them back to Spain to illustrate the savages they'd found in the new world. This "pick and choose" method tore tribal families apart. Second, families and tribes were placed on reservations. On May 20, 1830, the Indian Removal Act was implemented—an act that destroyed Indian cultures and societies by institutionalizing their forced removal from tribal lands (Marger 1994). The most notable removal occurred among the Five Civilized Tribes (Cherokee, Chickasaw, Choctaw, Creek, and Seminole) in the Southeastern states.

Native Americans filed two lawsuits challenging the constitutionality of the Removal Act: *Cherokee v. Georgia* (1831) and *Worcester v. Georgia* (1832). Even though the U.S. Supreme Court ruled in favor of the Indians, President Jackson enforced their removal using the Treaty of Echota as justification. This treaty, signed in 1835 by the Cherokee Nation, agreed to give up all lands east of the Mississippi River in exchange for land in Indian territory, money, cattle, and tools. Thousands of Native Americans, therefore, were removed from land they had inhabited for generations and placed on federal reservations (Thornton 1987). Many east of the Mississippi were forced to move to Oklahoma in the Trail of Tears (1838-39), perhaps one of the most devastating chapters in Native American history. It is to Native Americans what the Holocaust was to Jews, slavery was to African Americans, and internment camps were to Japanese Americans. Over fourteen thousand men, women, and children marched over twelve hundred miles to Oklahoma through Illinois, Kentucky, Tennessee, Missouri, and Arkansas. The relocation proved devastating. Tribes were divided, and over four thousand Native Americans died from exhaustion, starvation, illness, and severe weather.

Wars

Thousands of Native Americans were slaughtered or placed on reservations in wars against white settlers and the U.S. Army. The wars of the 1860s and 1870s were less than honorable (if there is honor in war), because women and children were slain not only during battle, but in surrender or times of peace (Sider 1987). Many whites echoed the slogan "The only good Indian is a dead Indian" as a battle cry to inspire soldiers before combat. For whites, defeating the Native Americans was their short term goal—long term, they planned to eradicate Native Americans and their culture (Bonney 2003).

To accomplish this goal, Native Americans were forcibly assimilated into white culture (though not considered equal). They had to dress like white men, behave like white men, and speak English like white men, condemning their own culture to oblivion by not passing it on to their children.

Furthermore, the Native American population and culture declined because of killings by military personnel, passage of discriminatory legislation, teachings by missionaries to reject their religious beliefs and accept those of the

English, and thievery of essential food and clothing by Indian agents. By 1867, the Bureau of Indian Affairs reported a "drastic population decline" within the Indian Nations (Bonney 2003, 144).

Ironically, during the 1973 Red Power movement, the American Indian Movement (AIM) instituted the takeover of a Bureau of Indian Affairs office building at Wounded Knee, South Dakota (Marger 1994, 171), where Custer made his last stand against the Indians in 1890. The Native Americans surrendered to federal authorities after a seventy day standoff that left two dead and at least nine others wounded (Jacobson 1984, 200). This incident focused public attention on the plight of the Native American.

Discrimination

Discriminatory practices have exacerbated the decline of Native Americans (Scott 1986). During the fifteenth century, when Europeans began arriving in America, Native American tribes controlled their economic, social, and political destinies. They considered themselves equals to whites. As settlers encroached on tribal land, violating treaties and condemning Native Americans for their "heathen" ways, Native Americans experienced psychological damage that has negatively impacted their self-perception.

Discrimination was the policy in the colonies, and settlers exterminated the Indians in what has been termed an Indian holocaust (Thornton 1987). Many discriminatory practices still continue today, however are somewhat more subtle—for example, allowing self-determination without providing the resources needed.

Native Americans have historically been forced to be something they are not. Not only were they physically defeated, they were forced to give up their way of life and adopt customs conflicting with their beliefs and norms. Their living space was limited to a specific circumference (reservations), and there was total disregard for them as a people. The resulting feelings of low self-esteem, hopelessness, and helplessness have exacerbated their decline (Sider 1987).

In attempting to rise above the generations of discrimination, some Native Americans have attempted to learn about their roots. They have become politically astute so as to capitalize on land and treaty issues. Gaining more capitalistic strength will provide stronger social acceptance, allowing them greater potential for self-determination.

The religious controversy over peyote usage can be viewed as a struggle to preserve a traditional aspect of Native American culture. The peyote religion is legally sanctioned, incorporated as a Native American church that supports the search for the old and the new by expressing brotherhood and prohibiting alcohol (Bonney 2003, 149).

Limited Food Supply

Massive buffalo slaughters limited the Native American's food supplies, leading to starvation. One non-Native American in particular, William Cody (Buffalo Bill), is celebrated by many Americans for his slaughter of the buffalo (Thornton 1987). His admirers make little or no connection between the slaughter of buffalo and the Native Americans' need for food, clothing, and medicine.

In 1922, the American Red Cross indicated that death rates among Native Americans had doubled compared to that of other population segments, and diseases such as trachoma and tuberculosis were common (Atteneave 1985). Inadequate food supplies, exposure to European diseases, malnutrition, and lack of medical care all contributed to high infant mortality rates and a further decline in numbers (Locust 1996).

Introduction of Alcohol

The introduction of alcohol by white settlers was also a major factor in the decline of the Native American population. Drunken Indians were easy to exploit (Axtell 1981), alcohol created physical problems, and medicine men were ill-equipped to ward off the evil spirits of the "fire water."

Alcohol is the most widely-used drug among Native Americans (Waters et al. 2002). Indeed, Native Americans are five times more likely to die from alcohol-related causes than any other segment of the population (DATA 2003, 7). While seventy-five percent of recreational drinking is linked to alcohol-related deaths, twenty-five percent is linked to alcohol dependency that also causes death. It has been found, however, that those who internalize their oppression and hold on to their culture and tribal identities are less likely to experience depression, suicidal tendencies, and alcoholism (Shusta et al. 1995).

Although limited data is available on treatment within the Native American population compared with other racial and ethnic groups (Garrett & Carroll 2000), Walters indicates that Eurocentric alcohol and other drug treatment models do not consider the Native American culture (DATA 2003). Treatments, therefore, may lack impact. There is a strong concern that alcohol abuse will continue to be a major social concern in twenty-first century policy discussions regarding Native Americans.

Contemporary Issues

Demographics

The definition of Native American will be debated for years to come. Census-taking among Native Americans did not officially begin until 1850 (Thornton 1987, 212); early numbers, however, were biased, because Native Americans were considered savage and uncivilized. They did not become U.S. citizens until 1924 (Thornton 1987). The census process, however, was flawed. For example, the 1860 census classified Native Americans into two categories—civilized (those who adopted white customs) and uncivilized (those living on reservations and holding on to tribal language and beliefs) (Thornton 1987, 213).

By 1880, Native Americans were classified according to racial purity. If pure or mixed with white, they were identified on the census with the letter "W"; if mixed with black, a "B"; and if mixed with mulatto, an "M" (Goldberg 1995, 240). Oftentimes census-takers did not bother to go to reservations, and it was not until the Census Act of 1889 that there was a move to include all Native Americans, including those on reservations (Thronton 1987, 213). Even then, many did not participate, and those who did often gave erroneous information out of hatred for whites.

Native Americans are considered a forgotten minority—they are the oldest minority group in America (Dinnerstein et al. 1990), and political entities who are sovereign nations. Sider (1987) suggests that the U.S. Supreme Court affirmed the non-minority status of Indians in *Morton v. Mancari* (1974). Native Americans can be distinguished from other racial and ethnic groups in America because they:

1. Have been in America longer than any other racial or ethnic group;
2. Did not immigrate voluntarily or involuntarily;
3. Have treaty rights that no other group has; and
4. Are not a homogenous group, but are comprised of many distinct nations (Bonney 2003, 125).

Demographic data helps determine the strength of racial and ethnic groups in society. The smallest racial minority, constituting only 0.9 percent (2.3 million) (Thornton 1998, 341), are American Indian and Alaska Native, while 0.6 percent (1.6 million), reported a combination of Indian and one or more other races. Combined, the Indian population is reported to be 1.5 percent (4.1 million) of the population (Ogunwole 2002). According to federal statistics, they are considered one of the most impoverished of racial and ethnic groups—they are poorly educated, school dropout rates are extremely high, and higher education is well below the national average.

Education

Native Americans' overall level of education, while varying among tribes, is lower than other racial and ethnic groups. In 1934, the federal government tried to boost Native American education by passing the Johnson-O'Malley Act, which made it such that school districts could intervene to improve the quality of education.

Studies indicate that drop-out rates are extremely high (Bonney 2003; Reyhner 1991; Scott 1986; Greenbaum 1985), a statistic linked to factors such as inappropriate testing, negative effects of tracking, lack of parental involvement, and irrelevant curriculum (Reyhner 1991). Higher education among Native Americans is also lower than the national average—15.5 percent of the population has a Bachelor's degree compared to only 7.6 percent of the Native American population, and nine percent of the population has an advanced degree compared to only four percent of Native Americans (American Demographics 2002).

Reservations

Reservations are Native American lands retained by treaties, statutes, or Executive Order. There are over three hundred reservations, the largest being the Navajo (Marger 1994). Many Native Americans exhibit a mobile lifestyle, moving between reservations and cities, largely because of their inability to adjust to urban life. Those who do make the adjustment, however, still attempt to maintain ties with family members residing on reservations.

While some are migrating to urban areas, "urbaneness" is also moving onto reservations. Thornton (1987) describes Native American urbanization in geographic as well as psychological terms—the moving between reservations and cities transmits urban social norms and cultural values to non-urban communities by television, newspaper, and radio. He contends, therefore, that Native Americans living on reservations have become urbanized. Other researchers would disagree, arguing that even though Native Americans are becoming urbanized, many still cling to traditional beliefs and uphold tribal customs. Native Americans strive, for example, to maintain their tribal language because many tribes decide who will be accepted based on their ability to speak the language.

The 1923 Indian Omnibus Bill focused on the individualization of tribal lands and the removal of federal troops from reservations. The 1934 Indian

Reorganization Act was intended to stop the loss of Indian lands and develop modern businesses. The 1946 Indian Claims Commission allowed Native Americans to sue the federal government for land grievances and treaty violations. As a result, four hundred million dollars in settlements have been awarded to Native Americans.

There has also been a voluntary relocation program designed to ease economic pressures and unemployment by relocating Native Americans from reservations to major cities. The Termination Act of 1953 called for the "rapid freeing" of Native Americans from dependency on federal support.

In the 1940s and 1950s, policies emerged emphasizing "termination," a severing of the historic relationship between the federal government and the tribes; tribal governments were abolished, and tribal affairs and resources were placed under state control. However, many Native Americans believed that the government's "real" agenda was one of internal colonialism—economic exploitation of tribal land, continued lack of economic opportunities on reservations, and cultural annihilation (Sider 1987).

Assimilation

Assimilation of Native Americans into society has occurred mainly through intermarriage. The government now allows tribes to determine who is or is not Native American (Thornton 1987). Many tribes have a constitution stipulating criteria to be met in determining who can become a member. Other tribes decide based on verbal deliberation by the tribal governing body. However, the 1996 amendments proposed by the Indian Child Welfare Act will remove from tribes the right to determine tribal membership, and might return control of Indian families to the states. If these amendments are passed, they will have a "severely detrimental" effect on Indian culture (Locust 1996). The Indian Child Welfare Act has been amended (The McCain Amendments to the Indian Child Welfare Act); these amendments are accepted by the National Indian Child Welfare Association and the National Congress of American Indians. The major provisions, aiming to keep Native American children in Native American communities and protect their heritage and their identity, include:

- Notice must be given to tribes and extended family in all voluntary child custody proceedings.
- Tribes can indicate their intent to intervene or oppose a placement within a specified time period.
- A tribe can intervene at any point if appropriate notification is not received.

- Criminal sanctions for individuals who conceal their Indian heritage to avoid the Indian Child Welfare Act (ICWA) process ("Support for ICWA," 1999).

According to Thornton (1987), Native Americans are more willing to accept the "Indianess" of unions with whites than with African Americans (many refer to the latter in derogatory terms). Even though offspring are often called African American, they struggle to maintain their Native American heritage (Thornton 1987). There remains the question of what to call these mixed groups. Off the reservations, they are improperly identified by police officers as Hispanic, or black. Many have retained their official heritage such as the Nanticoke-Lenni Lenope Indians, the Ramapo Mountain Indians, and the Lumbee Indians (Josephy 1991). Perhaps the most renowned of the African American Indian mixed groups is the Lumbee tribe of North Carolina, that the U.S. Government did not officially acknowledge until 1956 (Thornton 1987). Today, they have state recognition but not full federal tribal benefits, partly because tribal leaders voted against the Lumbees because of their open enrollment policy for tribal membership (Jamies 1995).

Worldview

Most Native Americans share a common worldview rooted in a spirituality that is evident in their religion, rituals, and belief system. They believe that humans are all related both to each other and to animals (Locust 1996), and that the tribe is greater than the individual. The earth is considered sacred, and humans are expected to act as primary conservationists. Children are taught not to destroy natural things without purpose, and if that purpose conflicts with the natural order, then the act should be reconsidered so as to preserve harmony (Shusta et al. 1995, 248).

Tribal women assume a subordinate role. Interestingly, however, the eldest female is the decision-maker in the family (Shusta et al. 1995, 253). There is also a great respect for elders. Wrinkles are a sign of life experiences; elders are responsible for passing knowledge and wisdom to children. Ancestral oral history is a phenomenon often misunderstood or unacknowledged. Ancestral spirits are said to possess powers that offer explanations about events in dreams (Locust 1990, 223). This is one reason that Native Americans become infuriated when anthropologists disturb their burial sites, as these are considered holy grounds where individuals go to communicate with ancestors who have passed into the spirit world (Locust 1990).

Because Native American tribes have historically been isolated, their families separated, different family and tribal members raise many children. Shusta (1995) discusses how Native American children have been taken from their parents and placed without parental permission or knowledge—a practice viewed negatively by mainstream society.

Enrollment and CDIB

Enrollment is the process of determining one's membership in the Native American community (Locust 1996). Membership is further acknowledged by the issuance of Certificates of Degree of Indian Blood (CDIB) (the "White Card") by the Bureau of Indian Affairs (BIA), a department of the federal government. The CDIB is the primary document used by the BIA and some tribes to determine tribal membership and eligibility for federal services. It identifies a person's "Indian Blood Quantum," which is traced from ancestors that appeared on the Dawes rolls (a product of the Dawes Act of 1887, the government's first major attempt to register all Native Americans so as to protect Indian land). As Native Americans registered, they were given 160 acres of land. Many, however, remembering past atrocities, did not register out of fear.

The Dawes Act pressured Native Americans to "Anglicize" their names (Anonymous 2004). Some view the CDIB as another means of degradation, as its application process entails tracing the individual's heritage back to the Dawes rolls—an effort that can be difficult because of name changes and because some non-Natives included non-Native names on the Dawes rolls to obtain Native land. Moreover, after obtaining the card, there is no assurance that the individual will be accepted for tribal membership because all tribes have different membership criteria. Some tribes, such as the Cherokees of Oklahoma, require the CDIB (Jaimes 1995), while others do not. In North Carolina, many Native Americans carry a card that specifies their tribe. Some view this card-carrying as a degrading control mechanism, similar to the passes once mandatory in apartheid South Africa (Anonymous 2004). Many, however, accept the card because it strengthens tribal cohesion.

Tribal affiliation is an important factor in defining Native Americans. Urbanization causes loss of unique social and cultural norms. Hoping to succeed in the white man's world, many give up their language—a practice that devalues tribal customs. However, many are taking steps to reaffirm tribal identity by maintaining contacts on reservations, developing American cultural centers, and raising awareness among tribal members about the hazards of alcohol and the importance of education.

Social and Political Actions

Native Americans have taught Americans the importance of patience, honor, and honesty. They have also become politically active. In the 1960s and 1970s, they protested over poverty, education, poor health, unemployment, and land issues. In legal cases, they claimed as Indian territory Alcatraz Island in San Francisco, and parts of Connecticut, Maine, Massachusetts, New York, Rhode Island, and South Carolina (Jacobson 1984).

Native Americans have also taught Americans the importance of the land—the discovery of oil, natural gas, coal, and uranium on Native American lands has not only renewed government interest (Marger 1994), but has given Native Americans a political vehicle with which to strengthen their bargaining power.

Buffalohead (1996) suggests that Native Americans continue to make political progress, as shown by the passage of two major pieces of legislation: The American Indian Act of 1989 and the Native American Graves Protection and Repatriation Act 1990 (NAGPR). The NAGPR Act stipulates protection for some burial sites, and outlines policies and procedures for the return of some Native American remains confiscated by organizations such as the Smithsonian Institution.

Law Enforcement and Native Americans

Most law enforcement officers, like most Americans, consider Native Americans homogenous, savage, uncivilized, alcoholic, and hostile. This is because American history books have portrayed them negatively, and Hollywood perpetuates the perception. Although many police departments require diversity training, few include Native Americans as a topic because officers seldom encounter a Native American in the performance of their duties. When officers interact with Native Americans, therefore, they often revert to degrading and disrespectful behavior.

Officers often misinterpret Native American behavior as hostile when they do not respond to such condescending greetings as "How" or "Me police officer...who you?" Officers do not realize that, in fact, it has long been a custom of Native Americans not to engage in "small talk" (Shusta et al. 1995); in their culture, knowing when to keep quiet is a virtue.

According to Bhungalia (2001), police officers and courts tend to ignore cases of violence involving Native American women because of alleged confusion between the federal and tribal jurisdictions. In other words, federal officers do not understand tribal enforcement and tribal enforcers do not understand federal enforcement. Additionally, she suggests that violence on Native American reservations is further exacerbated by federal apathy in law enforcement.

Tribal Law Enforcement

Native Americans have always had both a criminal justice system and a policing system. As of June 2000, the recognized tribes had 171 law enforcement agencies, and the BIA thirty-seven (Hickman 2003). Burton (1996) chronologically traces the Cherokee Nation's regulators who sought to control crime before and after the Trail of Tears, explaining how they implemented a law enforcement system and judiciary. After the Trail of Tears, the Choctaw, Chickasaw, Creek, and Seminole followed suit. Burton describes the Cherokee structured sentencing matrix: for first time offenders, rapists received fifty lashes and a cropped left ear; second time offenders, one hundred lashes and the right ear cut off; third time offenders, death. The Seminole Nation, the smallest of the five civilized tribes, had a different legal system—the chief served as judge, the council the court, and they killed felons expediently. After the civil war, many other nations created organized police units.

Native American police officers, or "light-horse police," did not have jurisdiction over whites or blacks—their role was to enforce tribal law. However, some of the light-horse officers were black and white. Former slaves who served in the light-horse police units were known as Indian freedmen. Native American officers were paid between five and fifteen dollars a month by the federal government, and received some monies from the tribes for special services.

Burton (1996) discusses the legendary Sam Sixkiller, Native American sheriff of the Cherokee Nation who became warden of the National Penitentiary in 1875 and the first captain of the U.S. Indian Police in 1880, a position he held for six years with forty men under his command. Sixkiller was also a deputy marshal and special agent for the railroad. As deputy marshal, he policed the streets of Muskogee and was killed in an ambush. After his death in 1887, Congress passed a bill making it a federal crime to assault or murder a Native American federal policemen.

Today, each reservation has its own police officers and its own methods of implementing criminal sanctions. Only U.S. marshals are allowed authority other than tribal police on reservations. If a Native American commits a crime off the reservation and then returns to the reservation, there should be jurisdictional cooperation. Many non-tribal police officers have difficulty identifying genuine Native Americans and, in some instances, non-Native Americans claim the heritage in order to receive reservation protections.

Native Americans and Crime

Little data exists on Native American criminal histories, largely because crime statistics on reservations have not been reported. Further, data cannot be generalized to all tribes because they are not homogenous and only federal crimes would be reflected. According to 1997 data available from the Bureau of Justice, however, most violence perpetrated upon Native Americans is by someone of a different race. On any given day, one in twenty-five Native American adults are under the jurisdiction of the criminal justice system (2.4 times the per capita rate of whites, 9.3 times the per capita rate of Asians). The murder rate among Native Americans is seven per hundred thousand, a rate similar to that of the general population. Arrest rates are lower for adults than for other racial groups, however more than double that of other races for alcohol-related offenses. The Bureau of Justice Statistics (BJS) also reports that the number of Native Americans held in local jails—1,083 per hundred thousand adults—was the highest of any racial group.

The National Institute of Justice's 2001 report indicates the need to address some of the Native American's concerns regarding increasing crime rates: 1) the lack of resources for law enforcement (e.g., training for police officers, adequate jail facilities), and 2) separation between the structure of traditional law enforcement and the values of the Native Americans subject to this law enforcement.

Stereotypes

Since their first encounter with settlers, Native Americans have been labeled uncivilized and unintelligent. Stereotypes are publicly sanctioned—caricatures of Indians are used as mascots by the Washington Redskins (NFL team), the Florida State Seminoles (University football team), and the Cleveland Indians (American League baseball team). Native Americans have not only advocated abolishing such derogatory images, but have voiced concern over the tomahawk chop used by the Atlanta Brave fans. The Inter-tribal Council of the Five Civilized Tribes, founded in 1950 and representing over four hundred thousand Native Americans, adopted Mascot Resolution #2001-08 in 2001 that banned the use of Native American pictures or symbols in sporting events sponsored by non-Native schools. The Council noted in its resolution that the use of Native American images perpetuated a form of violence against Native people that in turn perpetuated their negative self image. This action followed up the earlier action taken by the U.S. Commission on Civil Rights. On April 13, 2001, the U.S. Commission on Civil Rights called for an end to the use of Native American images and nicknames by non-Indian schools, suggesting that they promoted negative stereotyping.

On May 9, 1992, the U.S. Congress enacted Public Law 102-279, proclaiming that year as the year of reconciliation between Native Americans and non-Native Americans (Shusta et al. 1995). President Clinton also supported this reconciliation by suggesting the need to put aside differences so as to build "trust, understanding and respect" (Shusta et al. 1995). Until Native Americans are regarded as equals, they may not feel this same need for conciliation.

Behaviors that Can Cause Stereotypes

As Native Americans move into urban areas, there will likely be an increase in interaction with non-Native American police officers who misunderstand their customs. According to Locust (1996), the following behaviors can cause stress and conflict:

1. Eye contact. Sustained eye contact (for more than a split second) is considered disrespectful and hostile.
2. Bowing of the head. When someone of authority is speaking to a Native American, be it an elder, a medicine person, or a government official, it is appropriate to show respect by bowing the head. For many police officers, however, this action seems an indication of guilt, not respect.
3. Mother tongue. When under stress, it is common for individuals to revert to unconscious behaviors (e.g., a first language, praying, or cursing). Police officers, however, may think that Native Americans are plotting against them.
4. Handshake. Many Native Americans view a firm, vigorous shake as a rude show of force, bordering on hostility. People, however, may think them "wimps" or "fags."
5. Delayed response. As a result of past atrocities, Native Americans are mistrustful of law enforcement officers, and weigh all of the facts in a situation before taking action. When asked a question, they typically take six to eighteen seconds to respond, as compared to the Euro-American's average three to five seconds. Some officers interpret this delayed response as a deliberate stalling technique. The officer, then,

might react in a rude and demeaning manner by insisting on fast responses.

Summary

Native Americans constitute only about 0.9 percent of the American population. They are undereducated, underemployed, and receive poor health care. Since the first settlers entered America, Native Americans' rights and culture have been largely stripped, they have been treated as uncivilized savages, women and children have been slaughtered, and they have been separated from their families and tribes. Further, the federal government has violated, altered, or eliminated whatever treaties it made.

Some researchers are optimistic that discrimination will result in a better understanding of Native Americans' customs, values, and beliefs. It is anticipated that this will occur not only with a few cursory paragraphs in high school and college text books, but that there will be an ongoing, and mandatory, learning process for agents of the American criminal justice system.

Key Concepts

Dawes Act of 1887	Reservations
Genocide	Trail of Tears
Indian Removal Act 1830	Worldview
Lumbee Tribe	Wounded Knee
Navajo Tribe	Year of Reconciliation

Questions for Discussion

1. Explain why it would be difficult for Native Americans to forget American history.

2. Identify some dilemmas that law enforcement officers face when dealing with Native Americans.

3. Discuss why it is necessary for Native Americans (as opposed to the federal government) to determine who to accept as Native American. Provide examples.

4. The U.S. Government signed and broke many treaties with Native Americans. Discuss why and how these treaties might be relevant for Native Americans today.

5. Many factors have led to the decline of Native Americans. Discuss, and suggest ways to stop the decline.

Suggested Reading

May, P. 1996. Overview of alcohol abuse epideminology for american indian populations. In G.D. Sandefur, R.R. Rundfuss, & B. Cohen (Eds.), *Changing Numbers, Changing Needs: American Indian Demography and Public Health*. Washington, DC: National Academy Press.

<www.fbi.gov/pressrel/speeches/ashley102804.htm>. This is a speech made by a member of the National Native American Law Enforcement Association in regards to Native Americans and policing.

<www.nnalea.org/link.htm>. This page of links focuses on law enforcement and Native Americans.

<www.sgc.gc.ca/whoweare/aboriginal/eaboriginal.htm>. The Aboriginal Policing Directorate home page, the administration responsible for providing policing services to Aboriginal people off reservations.

<www.shadowwolf.org/tears.html>. This website explains and discusses Native Americans' long hard journey during the Trail of Tears.

CHAPTER 4

ARAB AMERICANS AND POLICING

Learning Objectives

1. Define terrorism.
2. Discuss myths associated with terrorism and the policing of Arab Americans.
3. Summarize the role of the Department of Homeland Security (DHS).
4. Explain civil rights issues relating to terrorists.
5. Gain a better understanding of the war with Iraq as a method of fighting terrorism.

Introduction

It is not the intent of this text to suggest that Arab Americans should be blamed for the 9/11 attacks. Rather, its focus is to demonstrate how stereotypes can breed discrimination and racism; criminal justice professionals can lose sight of their responsibilities if unaware of their own biases toward groups such as Arab Americans.

On September 11, 2001, nineteen Muslim terrorists committed the most devastating act of terrorism on American soil since Pearl Harbor. In 9/11, over three thousand civilians were injured or killed, and billions of dollars were lost (Anonymous 2002). These attacks were not the first by foreign terrorists in America—the World Trade Center was bombed March 17, 1993 by a Palestinian group.

Osama Bin Laden, believed to be the mastermind behind 9/11, has long been openly critical of U.S. capitalism, regarding America as evil and deserving of punishment. This is nothing new—Bin Laden declared war on the U.S.

on September 2, 1996, and again on February 23, 1998, because, just as the Afghan Mujahideen had defeated the U.S.S.R., so could Al Qaeda defeat the U.S. (Emerson 2002). Influenced by Abdullah Azzam, Bin Laden adopted the motto: "Jihad and the rifle alone: no negotiations, no conferences and no dialogues" (Bergen 2001).

Ultimately, terrorists aim to create an aura of fear by disrupting both citizens and the government. With bedlam entrenched, they then assert their rule over the nation. Although 9/11 instilled fear, Americans have continued to go about their lives, ever-mindful of those victims who died. In declaring a war on terrorism, President Bush continues to urge Americans not to give in to fear, and most of all, not to judge all Arab-speaking people by those who commit acts of terrorism.

What Is Terrorism?

Defining terrorism is a difficult task (Simonsen & Spindlove 2000), "sometimes as hard as the struggle against terrorism itself" (Ganor 2003). The FBI defines terrorism as "the unlawful use of force or violence against persons or property to intimidate or coerce a government, the civilian population, or any segment thereof, in furtherance of political or social objectives" (White 2002). While many opinions exist, there has been no consensus primarily because "terrorism to some is heroism to others" (Poland 1988). Schmidt & Youngman (Ganor 2003) surveyed researchers and delineated 109 definitions. Poland (1988) suggested that when defining terrorism there are two common characteristics, be they legal or theoretical: fear, and the achievement of some political objective. Fear, a powerful weapon, is a major component of terrorism. Random violence or specific acts against individuals are great tools for unsettling the masses. Political objectives can range from repressing political views and destroying social norms to discrediting and disrupting governments.

For our purposes, we will define terrorism as: A violent premeditated act or acts intended to create fear and cause harm to innocent individuals and groups in an effort to gain political, economic, or social influence.

The struggle for an authoritative definition of terrorism remains because of a number of unresolved questions:

1. How to define the boundary between terrorism and other forms of political violence.
2. Whether terrorism and resistance to terrorism are part of the same phenomenon.

3. How to distinguish "terrorism" from simple criminal acts, from open war between "consenting" groups, and from acts that arise from mental illness.
4. Whether terrorism is a sub-category of coercion, violence, power, or influence.
5. Whether terrorism is legitimate. What gains justify its use?
6. How to determine the relationship between guerilla warfare and terrorism.
7. How to define the relationship between crime and terrorism (Ganor 2003).

In the wake of the 9/11 terror, it is important that Americans continue to separate reality from myth. Walter Laqueur (1999) identifies eleven myths about terrorism:

1. **Terrorism is a new phenomenon with few historical precedents; there is little to be learned from what meager antecedents can be found.** Terrorism is not a new phenomenon, but Americans have only recently become aware of their vulnerability.
2. **Terrorism is the single most pressing issue on the international agenda, a "cancer of the modern world."** Terrorism certainly deserves high priority on the international agenda; however, nuclear and biochemical warfare are even more pressing issues. With the threat of war looming between not only some third-world countries, but the U.S. and North Korea, the focus has been on prevention. India and Pakistan have been readying nuclear weapons as their conflict escalates. Tension between the North and South Koreans continues to swell.
3. **Repression breeds terrorism: the greater the repression, the greater the likelihood of terrorism.** If we consider countries like China, long known for its intolerance for human rights and open repression of its people, this rationale appears flawed. When defining repression, we need to think in terms of human rights issues. Looking deeper, it appears that ideological differences can breed terrorism; the greater such differences between countries, the greater the possibility of terrorism.
4. **The only way to reduce terrorism is to redress the grievances that cause it.** Terrorism committed against the U.S. cannot be redressed because of the significant differences in ideological philosophies between America and the extremists.
5. **One man's "terrorist" is another man's "freedom fighter."** Laqueur suggests that, although some radical individuals may urge terrorists on in the name of their God, there is no unanimity on any position the terrorists might take. There is no justice in terrorists' causes.
6. **Terrorists are fanatics who cannot be brought under control until the conditions that gave rise to their fanaticism change in their favor.** Ter-

rorists can be brought under control. As an example, Laqueur cites the 1982 terrorist attack in the Syrian city of Hama. Though the measures used were extreme—leveling the part of the city where the terrorists lived—they prevented further attacks (Weigel 1994). This is not to suggest, of course, that such measures can be more broadly applied—the whole of the Arabic world cannot be destroyed in the name of controlling terrorism.

7. **Terrorists are poor, and terrorist attacks are a manifestation of the misery of the "wretched of the earth."** The terrorists involved in 9/11 had access to lucrative bank accounts, and spent large sums of money learning to pilot planes for the completion of their suicide mission. American intelligence has successfully tracked terrorists by monitoring their monetary transactions.

8. **Terrorism is the result of the Arab-Israeli conflict.** The Arab-Israeli conflict is only a small part of what has led to acts of senseless terrorism.

9. **"State-sponsored terrorism" has exacerbated the problem.** Though a number of countries sponsor terrorism by providing terrorists with arms, equipment, food, service, and money, other issues have exacerbated the problem.

10. **Terrorism can happen anywhere, anytime.** In effect, terrorism has been limited in countries ruled by dictators (e.g., China and Cuba). On the other hand, Saudi Arabia and a number of South American countries support this myth.

11. **Economic conditions determine the ebb and flow of terrorism.** Because terrorists of Arabic origin are responsible for 9/11, international focus has shifted to an examination of Arabic-speaking people and their culture. Arabs are individuals whose homeland includes twenty-two countries in North Africa and Southwest Asia. They are classified by the U.S. census as "white" or Caucasian, however they range in appearance from Latino to African American (their skin varies from dark to olive, their hair texture from straight to curly). As a result, they are identified more with nationality than with any racial group. Moreover, based on their physical appearance, they may be included in any of the five major racial groups. While not considered a minority in America, their physical appearance sets them apart from the majority.

Types of Terrorism

Researchers have described many different types of terrorism. Combs (2000) provides the following matrix:

Type	Committed by	Target	Tactics
Mass terror	Political leaders (e.g., Idi Amin)	General population	Coercion, organized or un-organized
Dynastic assassination	Individuals/ groups (e.g., Russian anar-chists)	Head of state or ruling elite	Very selective vi-olence
Random terror	Individuals/ groups (e.g. bombing of Pan Am Flight 103)	Anyone in "the wrong place at the wrong time"	Bombs in cafes, markets, etc.
Focused random terror	Individuals/ groups (e.g., PIRA and UPF bombings in Northern Ire-land)	Members of the "opposition"	Bombs in specific cafes and markets
Tactical terror revolutionary	Revolutionary movements (e.g., M19s attacks Co-lumbia Justices)	The government	Attacks on political attractive targets

Historical Perspective

Edmond Burke, a British political philosopher, first used the term terrorism to describe the violence in the French Revolution (1789–95) (White 2002, 67). Modern terrorism, therefore, is rooted in the late 1800s when Western European anarchists used violence to achieve objectives (e.g., the overthrow and assignation of the Czar in Imperial Russia). By the mid-twentieth century, this violence had spread globally—right wing groups in America were using violent anarchistic tactics (White 2002).

According to Laqueur, modern terrorists are more ruthless than their predecessors, using indiscriminate violence and intentionally harming innocent persons (White 2002, 75). Prior to the twenty-first century, much of the terrorism in the U.S. was domestic. Since 9/11, however, the focus is on homeland security against both international and domestic terrorism, and an increased concern about weapons of mass destruction (WMD).

Even prior to 9/11, Americans stereotyped Arab Americans as ascribing to a violent religion (Aswad 2003). The attacks perpetuated such thinking; the White House gave statements that suicide bombers had been religiously motivated, acting upon the belief that they would be rewarded in heaven.

Middle Eastern terrorism against the U.S. stems from political and religious differences. Bin Laden, a wealthy Saudi Arabian, played an instrumental role in the Soviet-Afghan war (1979-89) when the Soviet Union invaded Afghanistan. The Afghans, with U.S. aid, were able to force the Soviets' retreat. Shortly after, the Soviet Union collapsed—according to the Afghan Mujahadeen fighters, a sign of God's power over Satan (White 2002). Bin Laden, the victorious Mujahadeen leader, turned his focus to other nations he considered "foreign devils and infidels"—the U.S. and Israel—and called for all Muslims to rise up in a "Jihad," or Holy War, against "those things foreign to Islam" (White 2002, 162), officially declaring war on the U.S. in 1996. Because he called on all Muslims to fight, there has been increased scrutiny of Arabic-speaking people—they must now undergo a "special registration" process when entering the U.S.

According to the 2000 census, there are four million Arab Americans in the U.S., and the population is expected to increase to six million by 2010. Arabic-speaking people born in America come from many different countries. The majority are from Lebanon, the smallest percentage from Jordan. There is no simple definition of an "Arab" except to mean those who speak Arabic. Arabic, however, differs between countries (e.g., Jordanian Arabic is different than Algerian Arabic). Further, different ethnic groups within Arab countries might speak either a different form of Arabic or an entirely different language (Zogby 2002). While some assume that the Middle East is composed of all Arab countries (where Arabic is spoken), non-Arab countries exist (e.g., Israel, Turkey, and Iran). Although Iranians are ninety-five percent Muslim (Shiite), they speak Farsi (a Persian language).

Arabic-speaking people have emigrated to the U.S. in two waves: 1875-1920, and after the 1940s. Between 1875 and 1920, economic conditions caused the mass emigration of mostly Christian Arabs. Assimilation into American society was easy, and easier still as intermarriage rates with other ethnic groups increased. In the second wave, Muslims experienced difficulty assimilating because of their religious practices.

Islamic Faith

Both Christian and Muslim Arabs use the term Islam to mean Allah, or "believing in God." Christian Arabs believe Jesus is the Son of Allah, whereas Muslims believe that Muhammad was the prophet of God. Islam in Arabic means "submission to the will of God." Muslins have interpreted the Islamic religion as both peaceful and violent, teaching vengeance against its enemy. There are currently 1.3 billion followers globally; the closest religion to that in numbers is Christianity. As is shown on the graph below, only twenty-three percent of Arab Americans practice the Islamic religion (despite what the majority of Americans believe); the majority are Catholic.

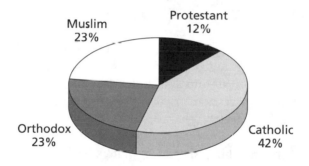

(Zogby 2003)

The Arab culture is extremely diverse—consisting of twenty-one states from Morocco to Iraq to the Persian Gulf, the Arab world includes over two hundred million people (Aswad 2003). When traveling between regions, one sees very different traditions and practices.

A central principle of the Islamic religion is the preservation of culture. Muslim immigrants' continued practice of the Islamic faith (children were required to study Arabic and the Qu'ran) drew unwanted attention, as their beliefs often contrasted with American culture. Muslins believe that life is controlled by fate; dignity, honor, and reputation are of paramount importance. The five pillars (obligations) upon which the Islamic religion is based are:

1. The confession of faith. Worshippers profess their faith with terms such as "in the Almighty name of Allah..."

2. Prayer. Followers are expected to pray five times a day from the Koran (before the sun rises, at noon, mid-afternoon, after sun sets, and at twilight).
3. Alms. Gifts to the needy (also referred to as "zakat").
4. Fasting during Ramadan. Followers must abstain from eating, drinking, smoking, and sex during the day (an hour before the sun rises and until it sets).
5. Pilgrimage (Al-Hajj). Worshippers are expected to travel at least once in their lifetime to Mecca to confirm their faith (El-Najjar 2003).

Historically, intermarriage between Muslims and Christians has been rare. Today, Arab American Muslims still feel pressure to marry within their religion; if they marry outside, the significant other is encouraged (pressured) to convert. Islam has been cited as one of the fastest growing religions in America (Aswad 2003). A challenge, therefore, lies in how (or whether) Arab Americans will practice orthodox Islamic law in American society. As is the case of many immigrants, each generation will likely assimilate into society, in the process modifying dress and language and culture.

Family has historically been important. Family members are socialized as a group based on patrilineally; extended family members emphasize "honor of the family and the rules and obligations of etiquette." Patrilineally implies inheritance or privilege rather than male dominance. Females (e.g., Pakistan Prime Minister Benazhir Butto and Indira Gandhi) also benefit from patrilineally. Still, males have more privileges because heritage is traced based on the father's kin (Aswad 2003).

Education is highly valued; eighty-two percent of Arab Americans have a high school diploma, thirty-six percent hold a bachelor's degree (above the national average), and fifteen percent hold graduate degrees. Further, Arab Americans are more likely to vote than many Americans, and hold public office at all levels of government—currently, there are four Senators, six members of the House of Representatives, and two Governors. They have held cabinet positions under Presidents George H. Bush, Clinton, and George W. Bush. Further, Zogby (2003) suggests that more Arab Americans have been hired in key staff positions as Democrats and Republicans vie for 2004 votes.

Three political factors have contributed to Arab American political progress (Zogby 2003):

1. Over the past twenty years, they have united under a common ethnic heritage;
2. They have mobilized into the political mainstream by becoming aggressive with voter registration drives;

3. They have the votes in "battleground" states like Michigan, Illinois, Ohio, Pennsylvania, New Jersey, and Florida. They are organized and evenly divided between parties.

Self-Perceptions

Arab Americans, like other ethnic groups, have brought a rich cultural heritage to America. However, they have also been portrayed negatively. As the war against terrorism continues, Arab Americans have become the victims of even greater prejudice. In reality, grounded in the Islamic faith, they tend to be generous, caring, polite, and loyal. Their demeanor, however, can seem otherwise. Aggressive behavior by males (crowding into lines, pushing, and aggressive driving) is deemed acceptable in the Arab American culture. Self-praise is common and even expected. They delight in discussions of money, religion, and politics. And while it is acceptable to inquire after families, it is not acceptable to ask specifically about women.

Arab American Rules of Etiquette

Some rules of etiquette are acceptable and expected of most Arab Americans. Nydell (1987) offers the following guide:

1. Sit properly. Sitting carelessly (slouching, draping the legs over the arm of a chair) when talking with someone communicates a lack of respect.
2. Stand straight. When conversing with someone, leaning against the wall or keeping hands in pockets is considered a lack of respect.
3. Hide the soles of the shoes. Sitting in a manner that allows the sole of one's shoe to face another person is an insult.
4. Shake hands. Failure to shake hands in greeting or departure is considered rude.
5. Share cigarettes. One who lights a cigarette in a group must be prepared to offer them to everyone.
6. Eat with the right hand. The left hand is not used to eat or take food from communal dishes, as it is considered unclean.
7. Do not photograph people without their permission.
8. Staring at others is not usually considered rude or an invasion of privacy.
9. Stay away from household animals, especially dogs.

Arab American Gestures

Both verbal and non-verbal communication is essential to interacting with others. Gestures, a form of non-verbal communication, can be quite misleading, as they mean different things in different cultures. Consideration of Arab American gestures, therefore, merits some attention. Nydell (1987) mentions important gestures, and they include:

1. Move the head back and raise the eyebrows: "No." Move the head back and chin up: "No." Move the chin back and make a clicking sound with the tongue: "No."
2. After shaking hands, place the right hand to the heart or chest: greeting with respect or sincerity.
3. Hold the right hand out, palm downward, and move it as if scooping something away from you: "Go away."
4. Hold the right hand out, palm upward, and open and close the fingers: "Come here."
5. Hold the right hand out, palm upward, and close it halfway: "Give it to me."
6. Hold the right hand out, palm downward, and move it up and down slowly: "Quiet down."
7. Hold the right hand out, palm upward, touch the thumb and tips of fingers together, and move the hand up and down: "Calm down, Be patient," or "Slowly."
8. Hold the right forefinger up and move it left to right quickly several times: "No," or "Never."
9. Hold the right hand out, palm downward, and twist the hand to show the palm upward: "What?" or "Why?"
10. Make a fist with the right hand, keeping the thumb extended upward: "Very good," or "I am winning." You may have seen Yasser Arafat make this victory sign when talking to the press.

Physical Contact

There are different expectations in terms of physical contact for males and females. A common public greeting is the kissing of both cheeks or embracing by the same sex. An extended handshake is common during short conversations. Hand gestures are often used when communicating, and it is respectful to make eye contact. First names are used; seldom do individuals refer to others by their last name. Women do not change their names after marriage, and interact freely only with other women and close male relatives. Any public display of intimacy between men and women is strictly prohibited. It is considered impolite to criticize openly, but praise is expected even if not sincere.

The clothing worn by Muslim women causes much discussion among many Americans who feel that, when in America, one should wear "American" attire. However, many Arab American and Muslim women opt to wear their traditional clothing, including the veil that covers most of the face. For most Americans, the veil symbolizes female inferiority, submission, and even oppression. Charrad (1998, 65), however, suggests that the veil also means "resistance, protest, empowerment and a political symbol." Different types of veils hold different meanings. The *safsari*, that implies tradition, is an all-white rectangular cloth that covers the body from head to toe. The *hijab*, that means "protection," covers only the head and shoulders. The wearing of the *hijab* is also considered a strong political statement of either empowerment, membership in a specific cultural group (or rejection of Western corruption), or protection against sexual advances (Charrad 1998, 67).

Arab Americans and Discrimination

Before 9/11, thirty percent of Arab Americans indicated that they had experienced some degree of discrimination. Since 9/11, this has increased significantly—in workplaces, schools, and among friends and neighbors. The greatest scrutiny and discrimination, however, comes from strangers in places such as shopping malls and airports (Zogby 2002).

According to Aswad (2003), the 1996 Anti-terrorism and Effective Death Penalty Act (provided for the deportation of immigrants even if they are not criminals) had a significant impact on Arab Americans. The law, according to Congress, would fight terrorism. An organization could be designated a terrorist threat by the Secretary of State, the Attorney General, and the Secretary of Treasury. Critics felt that innocent Arab Americans could become easy targets.

Many Arab Americans are concerned about the long-term effects of 9/11. President Bush even issued a statement cautioning Americans about discrimination: "Our nation should be mindful that there are thousands of Arab Americans who live in New York City, who love their flag just as much as [we] do, and...that as we seek to win the war, that we treat Arab Americans and Muslims with the respect they deserve" (Zogby 2002).

Arab Americans as Victims of Crimes

In the wake of 9/11, Arab Americans suffered a backlash of violence (murders, beatings, shootings, threats, and attacks on Mosques). A major issue plaguing Arab Americans today is that of racial and ethnic profiling. Profiling refers to the usage of one or more characteristics to target a subgroup. For example, law enforcement officers can, at any given time, stop and question Arab Americans who are Muslim, between eighteen and twenty-four years of age, and born outside the U.S. on suspicion of conducting terrorist activities (Zogby 2002). Society questions the use of profiling, and its success rate in crime prevention is debatable.

Following 9/11, scattered hate crimes were committed against Arab Americans and Muslims—fifteen times the number of anti-Arab crimes compared with preceding years (Human Rights Watch 2002). Incidents include:

1. Phoenix, Arizona. September 15, 2001. Frank Silva Roque killed Balbir Singh Sodhi. Roque was also involved in shooting at a Lebanese American in a store and at a gas station, and in a rampage of shootings of Arab Americans after 9/11.
2. Reedley, California. September 29, 2001. Abdo Ali Ahmed was shot to death after receiving death threats on his windshield.
3. Fresno, California. October 2, 2001. Rien Said Ahmed was killed at work after receiving threats. Four men were seen leaving the scene of the crime.
4. Cleveland, Ohio. December 29, 2001. Over one hundred thousand dollars in damage was done to a Mosque. No one was injured.

Congress, however, acted quickly to support the President's plea to remain calm and not discriminate by issuing a Concurrent Resolution on September 12, 2001: "Be it resolved that the Congress 1) declares that in the quest to identify, bring to justice, and punish the perpetrators and sponsors of the terrorist attacks on the United States on September 11, 2001, that the Civil Rights and the civil liberties of all Americans, including Arab Americans, American Muslims, and Americans from South Asia, should be protected; and 2) condemns any acts of violence or discrimination against any Americans, including Arab Americans, American Muslims, and Americans from South Asia" (Zogby 2002, 6).

The media, too, has played a major role in reducing widespread hatred and violence by participating in positive Arab American campaigns. However, the media has also been used as a weapon for terrorists, fostering many of the stereotypes (Combs 2000, 128).

Arab American Stereotypes

Although there has been a massive effort to reduce intolerance and violence, Arab Americans are still faced with stereotypes:

1. Orientalism. This plays on the historical East-West tension. Easterners were portrayed as barbarians, villains, and seducers of women, and were thought to experience torment between their Eastern culture and Western influences.
2. Oil-rich sheikhs. Although not all Arab countries produce oil and few Arabs get rich from oil, sheikhs are usually leaders of families, villages, tribes, or mosques. Rich Arabs are not always sheikhs and sheikhs are not always rich, however movies and television portray them as such.
3. Nomads. The media has also portrayed Arab Americans as nomads, Lawrence of Arabia types riding through the desert on white horses. Most Arabs, however, live in large urban areas—only Bedouins, two percent of the population, live in the desert.
4. Terrorists. Since 9/11, many Arab Americans have been targeted and placed under surveillance because of their ethnicity. However, President Bush was quick to stress that not all Arab-speaking people are terrorists.
5. Submissive women. Because of religious constraints, many Arabic-speaking women are thought to be submissive to men. However, women hold great influence over family matters. Furthermore, Arabic-speaking women are changing their patterns just as Western women did with the feminist movement; many Arab American women appear less in traditional clothing, and compete more with men in the job market.

Arab Americans have begun to establish national organizations that not only provide emotional and physical support, but work to dispel stereotypical myths. These organizations include the Arab American Institute, the American Arab Anti-Discrimination Committee, and the Union of Arab Student Associations.

Law Enforcement Interactions with Arab Americans

The FBI has classified terrorism into two types: domestic and international. Domestic terrorists are American citizens involved in acts of violence against the U.S. International terrorism, on the other hand, is inflicted on the U.S. by citizens of other countries. Prosecution of domestic terrorists might be possible using existing criminal codes. International terrorism, however, has no international criminal code, police, or criminal court (Vetter & Perlstein 1991). According to Wilkinson (1986), the prosecution and punishment of international terrorists should fall under the jurisdiction of individual states. This, however, would pose problems for state and local law enforcement organizations. In domestic terrorism such as hostage-taking, bombing, or hijacking, for example, the criminal could be easily extradited from one state to another (McVey 1997). When dealing with international terrorism, therefore, politics usually supersedes law in determining a course of action.

Law enforcement officers must deal with individuals whose actions are politically driven (White 2004). In addition, while state and local officers must participate in a collaborative homeland security effort, their role has yet to be defined (White 2004).

Anti-terrorism training for law enforcement officers is being offered locally as well as by the Bureau of Justice Assistance. The nationwide program, State and Local Anti-Terrorism Training (SLATT), offers training for state and local police organizations. Not only are police officers being taught how to work together and react in times of crisis, they are learning to become more proactive in seeking out and interacting with Arab Americans so as to learn more about them and their culture, and are recruiting more Arab Americans into law enforcement to establish better covert operations.

Arab Americans continue to experience one of the highest rates of victimization following 9/11, the suicide bombings in Israel, and the Gulf War. Law enforcement officers often consider them more perpetrators than victims. Arab Americans do not readily take their concerns to police officers, however, because they desire to keep family and communal issues within the community. It is difficult, therefore, for officers to secure information. Officers will have to become proactive in identifying those Arabic-speaking people who might be terrorists, while preventing Arab Americans from becoming victims. In this way, they might gain the trust of Arab Americans.

Weapons and Terrorism

Terrorists' weapons of choice have evolved from firearms and kidnapping to threatening the use of biochemical, nuclear, and other WMD. However, Osterholm & Schwartz (White 2004, 85) suggest that by placing all WMD in the same category, law enforcement officers are unsure how to respond to individual attacks. White has identified three categories of WMD:

1. Nuclear weapons such as atomic bombs and radioactive materials. Nuclear devices are relatively easy to produce by skilled scientists with the necessary materials (Clutterbuck 1993). Although many nations have agreed to destroy nuclear weapons by signing the Non-Proliferation Treaty (NPT), some (including the U.S.) maintain their nuclear arsenals and are being closely scrutinized by the UN's Security Council.
2. Biological weapons such as bacterial microbes, viruses, and biological agents.
3. Chemical weapons such as nerve and blood agents, choking and blistering agents (White 2004, 84-5), and the use of gas (e.g., mustard gas). Like biological weapons, chemical weapons are difficult to control because of environmental variables such as wind and rain that could facilitate the chemical traveling unchecked over great distances. Terrorists have used chemical weapons on their own people. Saddam Hussein, for example, used chemical weapons following a period of civil unrest in Iraq (Powell 2002). There is no reason to believe, therefore, that terrorists would hesitate to use WMD on other countries.

A forth category is cyberspace weapons, technological infrastructure attacks with cyber viruses that could harm telecommunications and destroy important databases.

Car, truck, and human bombs, historically used by the IRA, Arabic- speaking people, and Israelis, are considered conventional methods of terrorism. Car and truck bombs usually contain great amounts of explosives and are rammed into a building just before exploding. An individual may be driving, or the vehicle may be being operated remotely. Individuals committed to a cause also strap bombs to their bodies and enter structures, believing that they will be rewarded after death.

Law Enforcement and Terrorism

To react to terrorism effectively, law enforcement organizations must be prepared with a strategy to protect all American citizens. Bodrero (2002) has offered a model emphasizing proactive defensive measures by police officers:

1. Interdiction and prevention that focuses on training, intelligence gathering, and planning;

2. Crisis management, controlling a situation while in progress; and
3. Consequence management, emergency response activity after the fact.

Bodrero explains that planning and working collaboratively is extremely important to fighting terrorism. State and local police officers, therefore, must be aware of basic principles (what, where, and how), and be able to analyze and share information with other law enforcement organizations.

Because terrorists use a broad range of weapons, law enforcement must have at their disposal a broad range of responses, including cooperation, coordination of security, and intelligence (Kupperman & Smith 1993). As a contingency plan, the Bush administration passed the Homeland Security Act, which established the Department of Homeland Security (DHS), the fifteenth executive department in the Cabinet. The DHS, created in October 2001, is tasked with protecting U.S. citizens from terrorist attacks, and ensuring that the U.S. is prepared to respond to and recover from any emergency. The DHS maintains U.S. borders and transportation systems, monitors who and what (equipment) enters the U.S., analyzes, reduces, and recovers information, and maintains the flow of intelligence by coordinating law enforcement organizations around terrorist threats.

Tom Ridge was appointed (and unanimously confirmed by the Senate) as Secretary of the DHS. Since his appointment, Ridge has focused on strengthening aviation and border security, stockpiling medicines to defend against bioterrorism, improving information-sharing among federal agencies, and employing more individuals to protect infrastructure. This is the first time in U.S. history that an act has resulted in the coordination and sharing of information by federal agencies.

The DHS offers new strategies not only for securing U.S. infrastructure, but for reassessing and implementing state and local police units including (White 2004):

- United States Secret Service
- National Infrastructure Protection Center
- Energy Assurance Office
- National Communications System
- United States Coast Guard
- Customs Service
- Transportation Security Administration
- Federal Protective Service
- Immigration & Naturalization Service (selected functions)
- Office of Domestic Preparedness
- Department of Agriculture (selected functions)

- Federal Law Enforcement Training Center
- National Bio-Weapons Defense Analysis Center
- Nuclear Threat Assessment programs
- Federal Emergency Management Agency
- Domestic Emergency Support Team
- Metropolitan Medical Response System
- National Disaster Medical Center System
- Strategic National Stockpile of the Department of Public Health
- Nuclear Incident Response Team
- Bureau of Citizenship and Immigration Services

Taboos

In interacting with Arab Americans, it is important to understand the pervasive cultural taboos:

1. When discussing issues, there is a tendency to "adjust" or bend the truth. Criminal justice professionals might assume that the individual is lying.
2. Police officers should not ask Arab American women to remove their headwear, as this will be met with hostility (head coverings are religious). This has caused debate as officers claim that women use their headwear to conceal weapons and/or contraband.
3. Nodding the head generally implies "no."
4. Corpses must be consecrated by an Arabic-speaking religious leader. Police officers, however, must secure the crime scene and the medical examiner must examine the body before it can be removed. This can create tension between officers and families.
5. An individual at prayer should not be interrupted; further, the floor on which he prays is sacred and should not be walked on.
6. The Koran is a Holy Book and should never touch the floor nor should anything be placed on it.

Often, tension arises between police officers and Arab Americans because the officer does not understand the culture or norms. The Human Rights Watch (2004), therefore, continues to seek cultural competency training for criminal justice professionals. If officers are sensitive to behaviors, attitudes, practices, and policies, they will be better equipped to work effectively in cross cultural situations.

Civil Rights Issues

Civil rights are considered fundamental to freedom. With a war being waged, however, it is expected that some freedoms be denied or modified. What impact does 9/11 have on the civil rights of Americans, and more specifically on Arab Americans?

The USA Patriot Act 2001 (Uniting and Strengthening America by Providing Appropriate Tools Required to Intercept and Obstruct Terrorism) provides a legal foundation for the Iraq War. It provides broader governmental powers regarding detainment, deportation, and investigation of suspected terrorists, places more restrictions on Middle Eastern immigrants, and includes a "guilty by association" clause stating that an individual is guilty if he/she associates with someone who engages in unlawful acts against the government. This clause frightens many Americans who fear that increased police powers (secret searches and surveillances) without appropriate legal monitors could infringe on civil liberties (Zobgy 2002, 18).

A major concern of special interest groups such as the ACLU has been to ensure Americans of the balance between safeguarding constitutional protections and the elimination of terrorism. Americans have watched a detention center be erected at Guantanamo Bay to hold terrorist suspects. The detention center, under the supervision of the Department of Justice, currently houses about 540 individuals who are being held indefinitely (Jehl 2005). Many must endure questioning by the FBI if they originate from any country linked with terrorist activity. The ACLU has launched a monitoring campaign to ensure that Americans' rights are upheld throughout this process. It is important to ensure that prisoners receive appropriate care and attention, even during interrogations. Military sanctions have recently been imposed on personnel as a result of cruelties inflicted on some prisoners.

Another area of concern was the power temporarily granted to prison authorities to listen in on attorney/client conversations. Prior to 9/11, these conversations were considered privileged. However, to ensure that attorneys were not passing on terrorist information, the Bureau of Prisons temporarily granted permission for these conversations to be recorded.

The government has also sought to eliminate terrorist funding by seizing and freezing money sources. This has caused some concern, as many Arab Americans have been the focus of "secret and sealed" affidavits that allow for police officers to raid homes and remove items and property without notifying the victims (Zobgy 2002, 20). Since 9/11, many small businesses have been the target of secret and sealed affidavits as the government attempts to cut the money supply to terrorists and terrorist groups.

Attorney General John Ashcroft has implemented the Student Exchange and Visitor Information System (SEVIS), a new reporting method that allows for the tracking of foreign students. Many countries that support terrorism and terrorist activity also sponsor students to the U.S., encouraging them to collect scientific and technological information for use in terrorist activities. Some Iranian, Libyan, and Iraqi students, for example, attempted to gain information that could be used in creating biological weapons or germ warfare (Cordesman 2002). SEVIS mandates that all American schools report the number of foreign students, when they started classes, type of classes taken, grades, participation in school activities, and any problems they display while on campus (Zobgy 2002, 21). There is also an attempt to track and deport foreigners whose visas have expired, especially if they are Arabic-speaking or Muslim.

War with Iraq

On March 17, 2003, President Bush issued an ultimatum to Hussein and his family to disarm or leave the country. UN officials entered Iraq to inspect for WMD; however the inspectors received no cooperation from Hussein's regime. The U.S., Britain, and Spain viewed Hussein's actions as non-compliant with UN resolutions, and called for war. France, Germany, and Russia opposed the war and pushed for a delay. While the UN did not support the war, Secretary of State Colin Powell indicated that forty-five nations were participating in the coalition (Bumiller 2003).

On March 19, 2003, President Bush, with the approval of Congress, declared war on Iraq. "At this hour, American and coalition (of the willing) forces are in the early stages of military operations to disarm Iraq," he said in a televised address to Americans. U.S. and British troops struck specific militarized areas from the air and sea (Moore 2003), and Special Forces units entered Baghdad in search of Hussein and his family.

It was anticipated that this war would end quickly, because Iraq, weakened by the 1991 Gulf War, lacked the resources to withstand a prolonged conflict. Still, people feared that Iraq might use deadly chemical weapons (e.g., sarin, cyclosarin, and VX, a nerve gas and mustard agent); Hussein, however, continued to deny having such arsenals. After forty-three days of combat, the U.S. had dismantled Hussein's regime, and on May 1, 2003, called an end to major combat operations. As of April 2005, however, the U.S. and its allies had suffered over seventeen-hundred confirmed coalition deaths. Troops remain in Iraq in a peacekeeping role, and continue the search for WMD.

President Bush has characterized this war as "preventive," meaning that it would prevent the emergence of Hussein as a U.S. threat. His grounds for war were based on:

1. Hussein's brutal and tyrannical behavior as he engaged in human rights abuses;
2. Hussein's non-compliance to the UN resolutions agreed upon after the Gulf War; and
3. Hussein's future danger to the world order if he decided to use WMD (Kaysen et al. 2002).

President Brush also outlined the benefits of the war:

1. Removal of Hussein
2. Liberation of Iraq
3. Promotion of democracy
4. Enhancement of regional security
5. Increase of American power, influence, and leadership.

History will determine whether the Iraq War was a success. Some feel that the U.S. was not justified in taking action against Iraq, while others applaud the actions for restoring respect for U.S. power, enhancing the credibility of the U.S. military, and reducing the number of hostile forces challenging U.S. interests. Hussein's capture has accomplished one of the President's goals, however challenges still exist as American and allied soldiers continue to be deployed and killed. Indeed, many Americans wonder when the end will come.

Summary

Arab Americans will continue to undergo racial profiling until the tension between the U.S. and Iraq eases, and until Osama Bin Laden is captured. While the U.S. turned a silent ear to Bin Laden's calls for Muslims to kill Americans and Jews, there is now a heightened alertness. While Americans are trying to avoid a repeat of Executive Order 0966 (that placed Asian Americans in confinement camps during the war with Japan) and a prolonged conflict such as Vietnam, consequences are grave. Soldiers are dying in the Middle East, and there appears to be no UN assistance forthcoming.

As America continues to be targeted by religious terrorists, federal, state, and local law enforcement officers must protect citizens by proactively counteracting terrorist actions. To effectively conduct interviews and develop intelligence, police officers will need to understand the Islamic culture so as to be able to interact in Muslim communities—a complex situation given the diverse nature of the culture and law enforcement agencies' history of poor information-sharing.

Some continue to discriminate against all Arab Americans because of the deeds of a few. And some police organizations still do not share information. The coming years will challenge Americans, law enforcement officers, and the criminal justice system; the major challenge for all is not to repeat past mistakes.

Key Concepts

Department of Homeland Security	Qu'ran
Islam	Ramadan
Jihad	Secret and sealed affidavit
Muslims	Sheikhs
Nomads	Terrorism
Patriot Act	Terrorist

Questions for Discussion

1. Is racial profiling appropriate in dealing with terrorism? What are your thoughts about secret and sealed affidavits?

2. The U.S. Government is concerned about WMD. Have most WMD been eliminated? What countries still have such weapons? Should countries be sanctioned by the UN if they continue to hold WMD?

3. Discuss how the Islamic faith is similar to and different from Christianity (or another religion).

4. As students of criminal justice, discuss important factors to remember when interacting with Arab Americans.

5. Discuss different interpretations of the Qu'ran or the Islamic religion (peace vs. violence against the enemy).

Suggested Reading

Department of Defense. 2002. *21st Century Complete Guide to the Gulf War.* Washington, DC: Department of Defense.

<www.fbi.gov>. The official homepage of the United States Department of Justice's Federal Bureau of Investigation.

<www.nccj.org/nccj/nccj.nsf/subarticleall/354?opendocument>. An article posted by the National Conference for Community and Justice dealing with racial profiling of Arab Americans. Also a good source on community policing.

<www.washingtonpost.com/wp-dyn/articles/A21888-2004Jul28.html>. This is an article about several Arab Americans who continually have been abused by citizens after 9/11.

Chapter 5

Policing the Elderly: A Forgotten Population

Learning Objectives

1. Discuss the concept of the baby boomer and explain the social, political, and legal impact they are having on American society.
2. Explain physiological factors regarding the elderly that might hinder positive police-elderly interactions.
3. Discuss the "sandwich generation."
4. Explain some implications of the Crime Bill.
5. Discuss programs designed to protect the elderly.

Historical Perspective

Age impacts everyone. Like race and ethnicity, people make decisions based on age. Unlike race and ethnicity, most Americans will (directly or indirectly), experience ageism (discrimination based on age, a term first used in 1974 by Robert Butler).

Medical technology has greatly increased the average American's lifespan—those sixty-five or older are designated elderly, those between forty and sixty-four, middle-aged. While most aspire to live long, they don't realize the discrimination that they will face. Unlike Native Americans, African Americans, or Asian Americans, who have long experienced racially-motivated discrimination, ageism is relatively new. For those also part of a minority, the discrimination they already suffer becomes compounded. Most countries cherish and respect their elderly, and plan for them to live out their lives in dignity—America, however, has discriminated against and ignored its elderly, only recently acknowledging their plight. Still, some researchers feel that this may change with the aging of the baby boomer generation.

During the twenty-first century, the elderly population will grow from twelve percent to an amazing twenty percent. There are more citizens sixty-five years of age and older than there are adolescents. A person is deemed elderly based on three main factors:

1. Psychological age. This theory is based on the belief model: if the person believes they are old, then they are deemed old.
2. Physical age. This theory is based on appearance. While genetic history is a major determinant, many (especially the wealthy) are temporarily reversing the aging process with plastic surgery.
3. Chronological age. Certain events and behavior patterns should occur at particular life stages. Societal expectations are grounded in stereotypical thinking, usually based on cultural differences.

Factors Affecting the Elderly

Two major factors are important to note when discussing the elderly: baby boomers and the impact of immigration.

Baby Boomers

Baby boomers are those born in the U.S. between the years 1946-64 (post-World War II) (Dailey 1998). Boomers are said to have a style unique in their own right. They witnessed revolutionary changes in the legal system during the 1950s and 1960s as a result of major court decisions and policy changes (*Brown v. Board of Education* 1954 and the Civil Rights Act 1964). They witnessed a court system that stressed individual due process rights. They lived through the televised assassination of four American leaders: President John F. Kennedy, civil rights leader Martin Luther King Jr., U.S. Senator Robert F. Kennedy, and Nation of Islam leader Malcolm X. They participated in domestic and foreign affairs, protesting the Vietnam War. They marched on Washington, went to jail to protest treatment of racial minorities, sent messages expounding love, and tuned on and tuned out with drugs.

This group, which will reach age sixty-five by 2030, will be the largest generation of senior citizens in American history (Rosenblatt n.d.) and will comprise 16 percent of the population (U.S. Census Bureau 2001). While they have become more conservative with age, many have attained politically powerful positions, and thus will impact major decisions. They are concerned about family values as they struggle with the cost of health care services and parental care. They discuss crime, and fear the increasing violence. They are concerned about the war in Bosnia, the nuclear build-up in China, drug use and distribution, and whether or not their grandchildren will have a world in which to grow up.

Immigration

Immigration has resulted in there being different cultural views regarding the elderly. The fast-growing Asian American population, for example, respects its elderly as gatekeepers of heritage, relying on them for their wisdom. Few seek nursing home care, as the family is expected to provide. Because people have always and will continue to define America, incoming cultures will no doubt change the ideology, including how the elderly are viewed.

The Changing Role of the Elderly

The role of the elderly in American society has changed immensely because of: longer life expectancy, non-traditional roles, and changing laws.

Life Expectancy

Life expectancy refers to the average number of years a person is expected to live. Americans are living longer now; the average life expectancy for men is 73.2, for women, 79.8 (Riekse & Holstege 1996). This impacts the health care system, calling for a need to examine long term medical care. Because people are living longer, doctors are better able to study both debilitating diseases (the leading causes of death among the elderly are cancer, heart disease, and stroke), and physiological and psychological processes over the life cycle.

Longevity has meant that Americans now expect to live longer, and thus proactively strive to become healthier through exercise and dietary control—more health clubs exist than ever before, and consumers of all ages have begun buying foods containing no carcinogens, limited amounts of fat, and the Recommended Daily Allowances (RDA) of nutrients. Furthermore, preventive care has become the most common method of dealing with health problems. People make frequent doctor's visits, hoping to identify problems early.

Non-Traditional Roles

While gender roles have changed drastically with the Women's Liberation Movement, so too has the role of the elderly changed with the coming of age of the baby boomers. Twenty years ago, for example, a typical elderly person had gray hair and wrinkles, sat in a rocker on the porch, and babysat grandchildren. While today's grandparents may enjoy their grandchildren, they are also going out more to movies, bingo, aerobics, and singles' bars. They are even advertising for dates or companionship.

Furthermore, while grandparents have often raised their grandchildren, many now have the added burden of raising their great-grandchildren (as many grandchildren are becoming pregnant in their early teens). The "sandwich generation" (where middle-aged adults are caught between their children and their aging parents) (Roots 1998) is therefore becoming a "sundae generation." Problematically, this causes the family to weaken. The grandparents cannot provide wisdom because they are too busy managing home situations, and the family views the grandparent as part of the problem rather than a resource.

Another significant role change is in business. Today, more elderly fight to retain their status in the business world by changing their appearance with hair rinses, designer clothes, and surgery. Television and movies use more elderly stars—many soap stars, for example, are sixty or older and are portrayed as villains, business executives, and even lovers. The double standard that women become old while men become distinguished is outdated. Older women are increasingly dating and marrying younger men.

Finally, colleges and universities are seeing major changes in enrollment. Many are developing weekend and evening programs as more elderly are returning to school, proudly accepting the title of "non-traditional" student. Universities encourage their enrollment, as their life experience adds to the educational process by enhancing classroom discussion.

Changing Laws

Retirement can create stress and frustration, but also happiness. Many states have changed mandatory retirement laws. For example, no longer are people required to retire after age sixty-five. In the past, retirees would collect social security checks, engaging less in social and political events. A new breed of retirees appeared in the 1990s, called the "unretired retired" by Gibson (1987). These people want to remain active; they retire from one company and seek employment elsewhere (full-time or part-time), or retire and return part-time to the same company. Many work at fast food restaurants, have paper routes, or volunteer as counselors for troubled teens, people at drug treatment centers, and prisoners. Some (e.g., retired judges, college professors, schoolteachers, and nurses) are used periodically in their old positions as the need arises.

Legislation Affecting the Elderly

American society did little to address the problem of discriminatory employment policies until Congress enacted the Older American Act of 1965, the first major piece of legislation to design and implement programs specifically for the elderly (Riekse & Holslege 1996). It created the Administration on Aging (AOA) under the auspices of the Department of Health and Human Services, an organization that acts as advocate for the elderly by making the community aware of their needs and educating them on the availability of special benefits. The provisions of the act include counseling services, meals on wheels, visiting nurses, and senior citizen support centers (Hartman-Stein 1999).

The Age Discrimination in Employment Act of 1967 states that age cannot be used against an individual in the work force when hiring, promoting, and training (Aiken 1995). Riekse & Holstege (1996, 184–85) delineated the following provisions of the act:

Ability should be considered rather than age.

- There should be no arbitrary age discrimination in employment.
- Employees should work collaboratively in resolving problem areas related to age.

This act has been amended a number of times:

- 1974. Extended to government employees.
- 1978. Age protection extended to seventy years.
- 1982. Required companies to keep individuals over sixty-five on the company health plan.
- 1984. Extended to American citizens working in foreign countries.
- 1986. Removed all age limits, excepting college professors.
- 1994. Lifted the age limit on college professors.

Euthanasia

The medical community seems divided over the issue of physician-assisted suicide, whether it is humane to allow individuals to choose to end their life with dignity rather than suffering the ravages of a terminal illness. This concept was debated a great deal in the 1990s, primarily because of the work of Dr. Jack Kervorkian who assisted with over 130 such suicides. After three acquittals and one mistrial, Dr. Kevorkian was found guilty of second-degree murder in 1999 for giving a lethal injection to a patient suffering from Lou Gehrig's disease. Kevorkian, a believer in allowing patients to "go with dignity," built a suicide machine that he called "Thanatron" (Greek for death machine). With this device, his patients could simply pull the trigger to receive an intravenous drip of saline and thiopental (induces deep sleep) and potassium chloride (stops the heart) (Frontline 1998). Dr. Kevorkian is currently incarcerated in the Thumb Correctional Facility in Michigan, where he is ineligible for parole until June 1, 2007.

One area of debate is whether medical doctors have the right to assist with death when they have sworn an oath to save lives. While the Supreme Court unanimously upheld decisions in New York and Washington to criminalize assisted suicide, Oregon held out and passed the Death with Dignity Act in 1997. Other countries have legalized euthanasia and physician-assisted suicide (the Netherlands on April 10, 2001, Belgium on May 16, 2002).

Living Wills

Although people are living longer, some elderly suffer from terminal illnesses and disabilities. Some have drawn up living wills, specifying their desire to "pull the plug" if they reach a point where they've lost all brain function or cannot exist without the aid of respiratory machines. Living wills (also known as Health Care Directives, Advanced Directives, or Directives to Physicians), are written statements by the patient instructing medical doctors or other health care providers whether manual or mechanical life-sustaining efforts can be used.

Health Care

Medicare, enacted in 1965, is a form of health care that supplements financial portions of health service fees for the elderly (Scott 2001). Medicaid is another program where public assistance clients and the elderly can receive Medicare and Medicaid simultaneously (Cutler 1997). Both of these programs are supplements to the 1935 Social Security Act.

In 2003, President Bush signed the Medicare Reform Bill, a bill estimated to cost four hundred billion dollars over the next ten years that provides the elderly with "better choices and more control over their health care" (CBS

News 2003). The major portion of the reform provides prescription drug coverage to the federal health insurance program beginning in 2006, which means that elderly citizens can purchase a Medicare-approved discount card for thirty dollars or less to offset the cost of their prescriptions. Some other provisions include:

- A two year program to cover chiropractic services;
- A three year provision to allow Medicare to contract with private firms for "identifying underpayments and overpayments and recouping overpayments"; and
- Encourages insurance companies to offer private plans to the elderly who receive health care benefits under terms fixed by the government.

Health care, especially for the elderly, is a politically charged issue. While everyone agrees that something has to be done about its cost, there is disagreement about what should be done. Some politicians suggest that the reforms are not enough, or that they constitute a "sellout" to the drug companies. Other critics suggest that the reforms will effectively privatize Medicare. The general population also seems concerned about the high cost to the government. If one considered the elderly a resource to society, however, this monetary burden might seem justified.

Political Activities

Politicians continue to seek support of the elderly because the group is growing and has established a powerful political base with organizations such as the American Association of Retired Persons (AARP). Dedicated to the needs and interests of people fifty years and over, AARP lists its membership at over thirty-five million (AARP n.d.), making it the largest political lobby group in America. It advocates the availability of educational services to enhance quality of life. Its programs are carried out through a nationwide network of area and state offices, local chapters, and volunteers.

The Gray Panther Organization, founded by Margaret Kuhn in the early 1970s, also focuses on issues dealing with the elderly.

Stereotypes

Like every other minority group, the elderly face stereotypes ranging from physical to social attacks that Schlesinger and Schlesinger (1988) has termed "granny bashing." They are considered frail, and are thus easy prey for criminals. Many will not fight back as police officers suggest, but some become involved with Crime Stoppers and neighborhood watch groups. In some states, in conjunction with law enforcement, the elderly have taken to the streets to "take back their community."

Other stereotypes include: distinct body odors, senility, unable to live alone, uninterested in (incapable of) sex, rigid, tired, cranky, weak, and dependent (Schaie & Willis 1991). Like all stereotypes, these are factually ungrounded, and are representative of only a minor portion of the elderly population, if at all.

Police and the Elderly

The criminal justice system has proven negligent by treating the elderly as complaining community residents instead of clients of the system. Police officers are insensitive to their needs, whether they are clients of the system, victims, or community residents.

Clients of the System

The elderly are increasingly involved in criminal activity primarily because of increased longevity, drugs, and changing lifestyles. Because they have had a longer time to perfect the skills essential for productive criminal activity, they are able to teach others. Although the largest number of arrests of elderly men in 1992 was for driving under the influence, the top three offenses reported by the Department of Justice (1993) were driving under the influence, larceny-theft, and drunkenness. The illegal drug culture has increased the number of individuals over fifty years of age involved in criminal activity. Many original gangsters (OG's), for example, have come of age and remain involved in criminal activity.

The elderly face not only health care issues, but feelings of isolation and hopelessness. Their lifestyles continue to change in terms of social interactions, which can provide incentives for illegal criminal activity. Because many elderly have lived in their communities for a long time, they know everyone, including leaders. Gangs, needing information to determine whether the community is ready for infiltration, often try to seduce elderly citizens by promising money in exchange for information. For example, elderly residents may be requested to gather information regarding community events (time, place, attendees, and location). Some are used as "look outs" or spotters, alerting gang members to police presence.

As clients of the system, specifically as inmates in correctional facilities, the debate continues regarding health care costs. Not only do inmates suffer from the usual physiological changes associated with aging, but the psychological effects of incarceration can, over time, speed up physical aging. Some inmates (aged thirty to fifty-nine) believe that imprisonment slows the aging process. Galliher (1989) has identified the following supporting factors:

- In prison, there are fewer temptations such as illegal drugs, alcohol, and tobacco—all substances that cause long-term damage to the body.
- Inmates eat regular nutritional meals. On the streets, they would be less likely to eat regularly.
- Prison is considered a temporary state; inmates believe they can return to the streets and continue where they left off. This thinking provides them with incentive to remain mentally and physically active.

Senna and Siegel (2001) have drawn a parallel between the graying of American prisons and the graying of America. Krane (1999) reports that the number of inmates aged fifty-five or older has tripled since 1986—a shift that has resulted in drastic cost increases because geriatric inmate maintenance costs (e.g., caring for stroke victims, quadriplegics, inmates suffering from Alzheimer's, cirrhosis, and other age-related medical conditions) are approximately three hundred percent higher. Elderly offenders have the same problems when incarcerated as they would in the community—they are stereotyped, discriminated against, and abused by prison staff as well as by fellow inmates. They have special dietary needs, medical problems, and physical handicaps. They also feel the need for protection from more aggressive inmates. As more prisons are built, serious thought should be given to caring for the needs of the elderly inmates.

Community Residents

Some police officers act indifferent toward or taunt members of the elderly population (Senna and Siegel 2001). Because the officer has been trained to gather facts, he may forget that an elderly individual might need help moving, hearing, or seeing.

The elderly may blame police officers for crime. This occurs because they fear criminal activities that seem never-ending and violent, and see themselves as prisoners in their homes. They especially feel vulnerable around the first of the month when they receive their social security or retirement checks.

Generally, officers work better with the elderly than with any other diverse group. This positive perspective is due partly to the fact that officers realize that they too will eventually join this population, but also because they would want their own mothers and fathers treated with respect. They view the elderly as less threatening, easy prey for criminals, and in need of assistance. Moreover, because the elderly are aware of most occurrences in their communities, they often serve as an officer's eyes and ears. Some join the neighborhood watch or Crime Stoppers units and watch each other's houses and activities, identifying anything deviating from the norm.

Senior citizens are the only group that law enforcement has worked with on a continual basis. Seniors and Lawmen Together (SALT) is an example of such cooperation. SALT organizes when officials need elderly individuals to work with them in an advisory capacity, as volunteers in police units, in the neighborhood watch, or with record-keeping (Riekse & Holslege 1996, 467). Still, police officers interact most with the elderly in situations not involving violence or crime, for example when an emergency service is used or an endangered pet requires rescue.

Victims

The elderly are not usually victimized more than other citizens (Senna and Siegel 2001), but they do fear crime (Brillon 1987). This fear stems from growing old, rising crime rates, and witnessing criminal activity in their neighborhoods. These factors may contribute to some elderly having a negative view of law enforcement, as some, not understanding that the court system and correctional services decide about releasing offenders, might feel that officers do not do enough to prevent crime.

Further, some police officers fail to show respect during investigations. Officers may suggest that the elderly person's version of an incident is inaccurate because of hearing or memory impairment, despite the fact that the person might still be a reliable witness based on what he/she saw. Some officers might speak loudly to a person with poor vision, and some may even imply senility as rationale for not pursuing the investigation.

The elderly are easy prey to consumer fraud and con games. Thirty percent of consumer fraud is inflicted on the elderly (Riekse & Holslege 1996), and con people cheat the elderly out of their pensions with get-rich-quick scams or "sure thing" projects. Seniors may pay cash to contract for cheap house repairs, and never again see the person who promised to do the work.

Often, elderly victims may not even report a crime perpetrated against them because 1) they feel embarrassed, 2) they fear that the person will return and harm them, 3) they fear that unsympathetic employees of the criminal justice system will abuse them, or 4) they do not want their families to know that they were victimized.

Despite their fears, however, the elderly have lower victimization rates than other groups (Senna and Siegel 2001). This is due in part to the fact that the majority of the low- income elderly isolate themselves in their homes. As their population grows and becomes more socially active, their victimization rates may also increase.

Summary

Changes in the elderly population, specifically the aging of the baby boomers, will impact society legally, socially, and culturally. Hobbs & Damon (1996) speculate that by the year 2030, the number of Americans sixty years and older will double, and those eighty-five and older will triple. Not only will there be a great need for services (especially health care), but attitudes will likely change. Those once viewed as victims may become more politically powerful (especially in the current presidential race) by forming lobby groups like AARP. No longer will the elderly allow themselves to be discounted or ignored; closing one's eyes to them will not make them disappear.

Key Concepts

AARP

Administration on aging

Age Discrimination in Employment

Ageism

Baby boomer

Granny bashing

Medicare

Medicaid

Non-traditional student

Sandwich generation

Questions for Discussion

1. What social, economic, and political impact are the baby boomers having on society?
2. Discuss the issues (systematic and otherwise) facing elderly prisoners.
3. Extended life expectancy has made it necessary to consider issues such as euthanasia and living wills. What are some factors to be considered when discussing such issues?

4. Discuss some implications of physician-assisted suicide. What is your thinking about Dr. Jack Kevorkian?

5. Explain the significant of AARP. What impact has this organization had on health care in America?

Suggested Readings

Annas, G. 1991. *The Rights of Patients: The Basic ACLU Guide to Patient Rights* (2nd ed.). Clifton, NJ: Hamana Press.

Scott, J. P. 2001. *Age Through Ethnic Lenses: Caring for the Elderly in a Multicultural Society*. New York, NY: Rowman and Littlefield.

Smith, W. 1999. When death is our physician. *New Oxford Review*, 66(11) 26–31.

<www.aoa.gov/about/legbudg/oaa/legbudg_oaa.asp>. An overview of the Older American Act, its purpose, and ratification throughout the past 40 years.

<www.census.gov/population/www/socdemo/age.html#older>. An insight of the growing elder population in the United States.

<http://grassley-senate.gov/releases/2001/o01r5-7c.htm>. Discusses the month of May and how it has helped the nation focus on the contributions and achievements of America's older citizens.

CHAPTER 6

POLICING AFRICAN AMERICANS

Learning Objectives

1. Discuss the impact of slavery on African Americans and American society.
2. Explain the importance of the landmark case *Brown v. Board of Education*.
3. Explain the role of religion in African American families.
4. Consider the impact of the Civil Rights Act on African Americans.
5. Discuss issues facing African American police officers.

Historical Perspective

Slavery in America began in 1619 in Jamestown, Virginia, when slave traders enslaved Africans to work for whites because Native Americans were dying from diseases introduced by European settlers. The slave trade seemed profitable—Africans showed a higher immunity to foreign disease, and Europeans had already been trading goods such as copper, iron, and rum in West Africa (Frazier 1988). Business, therefore, expanded to include human bondage, which became the most valuable commodity. Involuntary immigrants became numerous and global; by 1850, nearly one third of people outside of Africa were of African heritage (Harmer 2001). Clearly, the colonists failed to anticipate the slave trade's long-term impact.

Enslaved Africans came from a wide variety of backgrounds. Many were of royal descent, and some had been prisoners of warring tribes. Whatever their previous status, however, they had never experienced such savagery as was inflicted upon them by their captors: "I feared I should be put to death, the white people looked and acted, as I thought, in so savage a manner, for

I had never seen among any people such instances of brutal cruelty..." (Frazier 1988, 12)

Initially, Africans were sold as indentured servants; until slavery became a legalized institution, there was little cruelty or inhumanity. Massachusetts was the first colony to legalize slavery in 1641; Africans entering the state were identified as slaves, and those already there were legally free but treated as slaves (Bush 2000). Shortly thereafter, other colonies followed suit, instituting Slave Codes to control Africans. These codes forbade the owning of property, mandated that travel be done only with a special pass, prohibited the carrying of weapons, and allowed marriage only with permission.

Africans adapted to their new environment and exhibited skills (e.g., artistry, hunting and tracking, and using plants for medicinal purposes); whites, therefore, felt threatened and limited them to agricultural work (Eltis 2000). Slaves gathered information using methods they learned from whites, in the process discovering their owners' weaknesses. And perhaps most importantly, slaves learned to use the courts to protest enslavement and gain freedom.

Use of the Legal System

One of the most infamous court battles in slave history was the 1857 *Dred Scott* decision. In the case, Dred Scott, of St. Louis, Missouri, filed a lawsuit to win freedom for himself and his family. Three major issues were involved: whether Scott, as a slave, had the right to sue, whether his residence in Illinois granted him freedom, and whether Congress had the constitutional right to prohibit slavery in federal territories. The Supreme Court, interpreting laws based on public opinion, ruled that because Scott was a slave, he had no right to sue. The Constitution did not, nor does it today, contain guarantees regulated by individual state statutes. Even though Scott lost, the case represented the first instance of slaves using the system to gain freedom.

Plessy v. Ferguson (1896), another landmark case, established two major factors: the separate but equal doctrine, and the definition of "Negro." Homer Plessy, a slave whose father was white and mother African, challenged the segregation of train seating in Louisiana. The separate but equal criterion stipulated that it was legal and permissible to use police force to enforce segregation—a decision that only got reversed in *Brown v. Board of Education* (1954). Because Plessy looked white, further, the Supreme Court took the opportunity to define "Negro" as anyone with known black ancestry in their bloodline (Harmer 2001). This idea led to the "one drop rule," that the smallest bit of black blood classified a person as black regardless of his physical appearance; a mixed race child was relegated to the racial group of the lower status parent (MacEachern 2003).

This definition served slave owners who were trying to keep count of their slaves, a dubious task as the numbers continued to increase (partly because the master-slave "etiquette" allowed white men sexual access to slave women under threat of violence or punishment) (Eltis 2000). This whitening of the slave population threatened whites even more; many felt that sexual intercourse with slaves was morally and legally wrong. To this point, no laws forbid sexual intercourse between African Americans and whites. To prevent any legal unions, segregationists got miscegenation laws passed in many southern states, stipulating that it was a felony to marry someone of African heritage.

Colonists used racial counts to separate Negroes from whites. Initiated in 1790, racial counting provided formal racial definitions as a part of the 1850 U.S. census (Harmer 2001). By 1890, the census requirements had explicit categories: mulatto (three-eights to five-eighths black blood), quadroon (one-fourth black blood), octoroon (one-eighth or any trace of black blood), and black (three-fourths or more black blood) (Gauthier 2002). These distinctions began to collapse in the 1900s when Negroes came to be considered any person with a drop of black blood.

Search for Freedom

Slaves used many strategies to gain freedom. Slave insurrections were commonplace, the most famous led by Gabriel Prosser in Richmond, Virginia, in 1800, Denmark Vesey in Charleston, South Carolina, in 1822, and Nat Turner in Southampton, Virginia, in 1831. Slaves also became involved in conflicts between warring groups (e.g., between Indians and whites, the 1770 Boston Massacre, and the 1777 War for American Independence). Often, slaves would escape—some joined Indian tribes, some headed north, and some joined the Underground Railroad. Many, however, were captured and punished with castration, flogging, hanging, or shooting. Slaves also used non-cooperation, earning a reputation for being lazy and useless; the slaves, willing to die for freedom, had faith that they would be liberated into eternal happiness in the next life.

Reconstruction

Lincoln signed the Emancipation Proclamation on January 1, 1863 out of political astuteness; in reality, he was intensely opposed to social and political equality for slaves. He proposed a "Back-to-Africa" movement that he called a "colonization plan" (Harmer 2001)—if blacks left the country, the Civil War would end without upsetting whites. The scheme proved inadequate because not only was it unacceptable to blacks (the second generation, born in the U.S., considered America their home), but to many whites.

Many historians consider the period after emancipation the most arduous in African American history as they struggled to exist and become citizens. Still, considering their previous oppression, their gains were enormous— rapid population growth, increased knowledge, and most importantly, their recognition as a powerful subculture.

The Reconstruction Period proved equally as difficult, but it allowed newly freed African Americans to study the system from a different perspective. For the first time, they could participate in the political arena; sixteen African American men won seats in the U.S. Congress, and many state legislative bodies allowed African American men to participate in their assemblies.

Several great men emerged during this period. Frederick Douglass, considered one of the most militant African Americans of his time, served as an ambassador. Booker T. Washington was considered one of the most powerful African Americans to enter politics because he acted as a catalyst for unified black/white support. W.E.B. Dubois, the first African American man to receive a Ph.D. from Harvard University, founded the Niagara Movement in 1905 to protest discrimination and build the African American voting machine. In 1910, this organization became the National Association for the Advancement of Colored People (NAACP), aimed at providing legal work for African Americans, gaining freedom and resources through the court system, becoming involved in the legislative process, and keeping the public aware of discriminatory practices (Harmer 2001). Marcus Garvey's organization, the Universal Negro Improvement Association and African Communities, gained prominence by espousing Lincoln's Back-to-Africa idea. Garvey claimed that African Americans would never receive justice in America because of their color, so they should return to the homeland where they would be treated with dignity.

The Harlem Renaissance, a group of African American intellectuals, artists, and professionals who joined to fight injustice, believed in Garvey's approach. African American art, poetry, dance, and music flourished as a means of self-expression, and family and church became used as survival mechanisms.

Legal Discrimination

Just when the Reconstruction Period seemed to have brought gains, the social and political rules changed, and African Americans encountered a new form of discrimination—legal discrimination (Harmer 2001).

When African Americans began using the Civil Rights Act of 1875 (that declared segregation in public accommodations and transportation illegal) to fight in court, whites changed the rules—on October 15, 1883, the Supreme Court declared that "the Civil Rights Act of 1875 was unconstitutional on the grounds that the Fourteenth Amendment does not prohibit individual discrimination." Rights contained in the Bill of Rights are incorporated into the states through the equal protection and due process clause of the Fourteenth Amendment.

Individuals and groups began to work to strike down as many of these laws as possible. A major twentieth century landmark case, *Brown v. Board of Education* (1954), struck down the *Plessy* decision and mandated the integration of schools. The 1964 Civil Rights Act, while a mirror to the 1875 Civil Rights Act, was deemed constitutional. There have been several amendments to the act since.

African American Family

Much has been written about African American families, ranging from negative "pathologicalness" as discussed by D.P. Moynihan to a positive expression of their strengths as discussed by R.B. Hill and A. Billingsley. From whichever perspective, the African American family has exhibited stability during periods of physical and psychological trauma—matriarchal design, disclosure patterns, extended family, and the church have all remained constant.

According to the 2000 census, 36.4 million (or 12.9 percent of the population) were African American or black (referring to individuals with origins in any of the black groups of Africa) (McKinnon 2001). And while respondents were able to identity their own racial heritage, 12.3 of the 12.9 percent reported themselves as black or African American while only 0.8 percent (1.8 million) reported being black as well as at least one other race. The African American population is concentrated in the South (over fifty-three percent); nineteen percent live in the Midwest, eighteen percent in the Northeast, and ten percent in the West. Detroit has the largest proportion of African Americans (eighty-three percent), then Philadelphia with forty-four percent and Chicago with thirty-eight percent (McKinnon 2001).

Matriarchal Design

African American women emerged as matriarchs out of necessity. Before Africans were brought to the Americas, their family unit was patriarchal—the man protected the wife and children, and provided food and shelter. Conversely, women cooked and cared for the family. Upon enslavement, these roles reversed, men taking on menial tasks so as to appear less threatening to slave owners. If a man tried to take on more, he was punished with whipping or castration, or else he was sold. Women, therefore, became dominant in providing for the family.

Men still take a back seat role in African American families—a strategy that has taken a toll on their psyches. It is still difficult, for example, for men to get jobs or gain admission into schools of higher education than for women with identical credentials (except if he is a gifted athlete). It is much easier, however, for men to be incarcerated—boys are even taught how to respond to police contact. Men have taken steps to maintain some balance of psyche—Louis Farrakhan's 1994 Million Man March in Washington DC, for example, was a counter-strategy used in their struggle for survival.

African American women were early feminists, as they always had to work hard for the family's survival. These women, however, have experienced degradation in many forms; the welfare system, for example, is a contemporary method of degrading African American men. Although statistical research indicates that the majority of recipients are not African American, many whites associate welfare primarily with African Americans. Consequently, welfare laws have been designed to perpetuate the separation of families. In the 1950s and 1960s, only single or widowed women could receive assistance. Many of the criteria today are designed to assist women while few services are provided specifically for men.

Extended Family

The African family provides food, shelter, and protection for relatives and family members. Many echo the Ghanaian proverb "It takes a village to raise a child," meaning that the responsibility of passing on ancestral heritage to the next generation belongs to the community.

To maintain and promote the extended family, African Americans strive to keep information channels open within the community by printing their own newspapers. While the dominant (white) newspaper may omit specific cultural components in a story, African American newspapers and journals include implications for their own communities.

From a Eurocentric perspective, the concept of the extended family has been difficult to understand. With slavery as a common bond, all African Americans are considered the extended family regardless of their socioeconomic status. It is not unusual, therefore, for African Americans to embrace others whom they meet for the first time; nor is it unusual for African Americans to assist others when they are clearly a minority. On the other hand, some isolate themselves as a coping mechanism, because they find it too painful to re-live the pain and struggle experienced by their people.

Disclosure Patterns

Whites in authority often consider young African Americans hostile and uncooperative because they do not readily divulge personal information. When criminal justice students question the causes of this hostility, they fail to understand that the slave system still permeates; it is not so easy for African Americans to forget the past. Indeed, because slaves were punished or killed when they offered information, children learned that certain information should not leave the home and community. Punishment continued in contemporary society—when social workers asked questions, funds were withdrawn or children were removed from families; when law enforcement officers asked questions, parents were arrested; and when teachers asked questions, other children laughed. African American children, therefore, fear answering questions about family. Disclosure of personal information is considered taboo.

As slaves, African Americans devised methods of passing messages or planning revolts without the slave owner understanding. One such method was through song. At the time, it was considered taboo to divulge methods of communicating revolts to slave masters. Today, messages are still sent via song; the rap and hip hop genres have exploded. The songs still contain elements of hopelessness, anger, frustration, and fear.

Another taboo within African American homes is the mixing of races. As was previously discussed, the whitening of the slave population caused concern among the colonists. Physical appearance was often misleading, and for a number of reasons, African Americans did not want to divulge racial information. First, they needed African Americans to gather information. Second, they did not want the slave owner to claim any children. Finally, admitting to having been raped would be embarrassing.

Today, biracial children are demanding that they not have to choose between races, but that they are allowed to identify themselves as multiracial or multiethnic. The Association of Multiethnic Americans (AMEA) was founded in 1988 to gain government recognition and political input (Fernandez 1995). Opponents of this re-categorization feel that it could devastate minority communities, make it more difficult to enforce civil rights laws, and complicate data collection techniques (Tessman 1999).

The Church

Africans came from many religious backgrounds, except Christianity. Whites did not want them to become believers for fear they would use Christian beliefs to gain freedom. Africans, however, sought to understand the religion on which colonists placed such emphasis. By the end of the century, separate African American religious societies were emerging.

Emancipated slaves soon realized that their freedom was based on a concept (Bill of Rights) that, for them, did not exist. They surmised that if they combined their African philosophy (Afrocentric world view) with that of the colonists (Eurocentric world view), they would be a much stronger people. Groups of freed Negroes, therefore, began advocating the abolition of slavery. Groups emerged such as the African society founded by Richard Allen and Absalom Jones in 1787, followed by the African Society in 1796. These organizations provided African Americans with a voice, and promoted the reading and writing of English. With some reluctance, Africans gave up their tribal languages to establish a common means of communicating.

By the end of the eighteenth century, slavery had been abolished in most northern states. This was not the case in most southern states, however, for two reasons: the invention of the cotton gin, and the Louisiana Purchase of 1803 (Harmer 2001). Excellent field hands, slaves were the backbone of the profitable southern plantation system (Eltis 2000). The Louisiana Purchase added land to the South, thereby increasing its economic and political power relative to other states.

Consequently, slaves contributed enormously to building American society. Still, their constant search for freedom is considered their greatest challenge (Alexander 1888). Their search for freedom guided and inspired other groups during times of oppression, demonstrated their creative nature (e.g., using song and dance to relay messages), demonstrated the use of combat strategies by civilians in getting to know the enemy and using his tools, and developed their tenacity in believing that they could overcome all odds.

Stereotypes

There has been a decline in the blatant stereotyping of African Americans as lazy, shiftless, immoral, and unintelligible. This shift could be due to the fact that African Americans have gained economic and political power. African Americans embody a real dilemma for America—while the country enslaved this segment of the population for two hundred years (and even after physical enslavement ended, psychological enslavement described by Wilson (1990) has persisted), it claims to stand for human rights. Furthermore, while scholars such as Murray & Herrinstein (1994), Rushton (1999), Shockley & Pearson (1992), and Jensen (1998) argue that African Americans are intellectually limited because of their inferior brains, many hold important positions—National Security Advisor Dr. Condolezza Rice and Secretary of State Colin Powell, for example, both advise the President, and Oprah Winfrey tops a long list of wealthy African Americans. These people have played major roles in eliminating stereotypes, but have also created yet another dilemma for America in terms of racial identity.

In early America, racial identity was simple—an individual was classified black, white, or Indian. With the increased immigration resulting from the drug war, the Vietnam War, and the Iraq War, the country has become more multicultural; today, it is often difficult to determine an individual's racial identity. The new racial category, multiethnic, used for the first time in the 2000 census, demonstrates this diversity. Citizens are now able to categorize their race as one or another or a combination of several. This categorization will prove a real challenge for law enforcement; while race has always played a large role in locating suspects and solving crimes, a multiethnic suspect could mean a number of combinations (e.g., white/African American/Asian, African American/non-Hispanic/white, Hispanic/African American/Native American, or Arab/Hispanic non-white/African American).

The U.S. Hispanic population has nearly doubled since the last census. Many have emigrated to escape turmoil in their South/Central American countries, Vietnamese have fled communist rule, and Middle Easterners have fled the war in Iraq. While some argue that these immigrants have made it possible for African Americans to become less conspicuous, others claim the opposite, that it is now easier for society to incarcerate African Americans (Wilson 1990) as other minorities can replace them.

Law Enforcement

Hostility and mistrust have always existed between African Americans and police officers. This is because police enforced slavery, conducted lynchings and castrations, upheld school segregation, enforced anti-voting rights, and controlled riots. According to Dulaney (1996), African Americans have always been policed.

Slave patrol was the first police system that set the pattern for policing African Americans (Dulaney 1996). The slave patrol worked in cooperation with paramilitary anti-black organizations such as the Ku Klux Klan. Homes and churches were bombed simply because the residents and worshippers were African American. Often, the police participated, or did little to bring the perpetrators to justice. As Alexander (1988) reports: "Little was done by law enforcement authorities to control the whites until blacks began to arm themselves and fight back."

In the twentieth century, frustrated with the unjust system, African Americans began to riot against the systemic problems. 1910 proved the turning point in race relations with the creation of the National Association for Colored People (NAACP) (Harmer 2001). It was a time of discovery during which African Americans sought to bring about change in a diverse society. Black intellectuals such as DuBois, recognizing the strength in collective bargaining, formed the NAACP with the goal of the elimination of social injustices. Because of his efforts, other organizations emerged—the Urban League in 1911, the Congress on Racial Equality in 1942, the Southern Christian Leadership Conference in 1957, and the Student Non-Violent Coordinating Committee in 1960.

Called the "black exodus," black families migrated north to escape the racial violence (e.g., lynchings, cross burnings) and other hardships (e.g., unemployment, illiteracy) in the south. The notion that things would be better up north was soon dispelled as families discovered urban ghettos rather than streets paved with opportunity. Martin L. King's non-violence preaching only exacerbated frustration, hostility, and anger.

Finally, it was an angry and tired Rosa Parks—called the Mother of the Civil Rights Movement—who demonstrated to the world how non-violence could bring about social change. The incident occurred in 1955 in Montgomery, Alabama when Parks was ordered to give her seat on the city bus to a white person. She refused, the police were called, and she was arrested. This incident triggered a bus boycott that completely changed the fabric of race relations in America.

Not only did King play an instrumental role in the planning of the bus boycott that lasted 381 days, but he set the tone for the Civil Rights Movement that eventually led to the passage of the Civil Rights Act of 1957 that created the Civil Rights Department within the Department of Justice, focused on allowing blacks to vote without fear of intimidation or retaliation, and the Civil Rights Act of 1964 that forbade racial discrimination by businesses.

The Civil Rights Movement created even more tension between the races because individuals had to adjust to changes (discriminatory practices). Many law enforcement officers, especially in southern states, had come from slave-owning families; now the federal government was requiring local, county, and state officers to enforce laws contradictory to what had been the southern norm. Churches and the Women's Political Council (WPC) played major roles in acting as liaison between the community and law enforcement (Brown 2003) in an effort to ease the tension.

The Social Context of Police/Community Relations

In the 2000 census, there were 36.4 million (12.9 percent) African Americans (McKinnon 2001). Interactions with police, however, still foster apprehension; each views the other with a stereotypical perspective. Complaints have included reports of racial slurs, abusive treatment during arrest, and police officers looking the other way. Still, African Americans consider police officers a necessary evil to maintaining social order. Consequently, residents must tolerate the continued abuse and cruelty extended by many police officers patrolling their neighborhoods.

Some white police officers become frustrated in African American communities when few citizens provide information to aid in investigations. This is partially because some officers present a condescending attitude; when officers work in partnership with community residents, they are generally more successful.

Often, police officers misunderstand African American communication patterns. For example, African Americans have been characterized as emotional. Conversation can reach a level of intensity that officers falsely perceive to be hostile. Because African Americans' fervor sometimes changes the sound of the language, many white officers perceive this as a sign of lack of intelligence. But African American language has evolved from slavery—slaves from different tribes developed a dialect so that they could understand each other, then coded it (and body language) so slave owners could not understand.

Many non-African American police officers cannot understand why African Americans can refer to each other as "nigger" or "mah nig" (short for my nigger, my man), while such terms are unacceptable when used by others. Detective Mark Fuhrman, for example, was criticized for his use of "nigger" during the *Simpson* trial. The terms are used both positively and negatively within the African American community—negatively in anger, and positively, implying love or fellowship—and accomplish two goals: self-definition, and a psychological coping strategy to deal with the terms being used negatively.

Clothing and manner of dress are further means of communication and self-definition. Some police officers believe that all youth wearing baggy clothing are involved in delinquent activity, when they may simply be expressing themselves. The oversized jeans worn to sport the "grunge" look, for example, was viewed as a sign that the individual was packing (carrying weapons and/or drugs). Oversized clothing, however, has become a fashion statement by African American youths who do not want to be defined by dominant society.

Issues of Racial Identity

Unlike other immigrant groups, African Americans entered America in shackles. Society called them "slaves," then "niggers," both terms implying inferiority and submissiveness. During the nineteenth century, they were called "colored"; and later in the same century, "Negro." During the 1960s and 1970s, African Americans no longer allowed mainstream definitions to prevail. The Civil Rights Movement was in full swing, and conflict with police raged as officers used attack dogs, batons, and fire hoses to control crowds. Stokely Carmichael (a.k.a. Kuwame Ture) called for "Black Power," a term used by African Americans as their experience took on new meaning (Black is Beautiful).

As American immigration policies relaxed during the 1960s, increasing numbers of immigrants entered the country. By the 1980s, it became more difficult for African Americans to determine who was black. In the late 1980s, Jesse Jackson, founder of the Rainbow Coalition, defended their right to define themselves as African Americans.

There are many black hues in society today (e.g., Jamaican, Haitians, Cubans, Arabs, Asian Indians, and Hispanics). It is essential in law enforcement, therefore, to know who you are dealing with. While a Jamaican may look like an African American, major cultural differences exist between the groups. While "in your face" tactics seem aggressive to African American men, for example, Jamaican men find them less aggressive.

Civilian Review Boards

African American communities have defended the need for civilian review boards to monitor police activity, because they have been victims of brutality and harassment more often than other minorities. As a result of civilian review board actions, many police organizations are now recruiting African American officers. These officers face a double jeopardy situation—discrimination at work as many white colleagues consider them incompetent, and rejection by African Americans for being sell-outs. In reality, because they are gainfully employed, African American officers often strive to be role models. Either way, they must live between two psychological worlds, which can be a devastating experience.

Specific Interactions

When interacting with African Americans, a person in authority should consider the following:

1. African Americans may appear emotional, but this is not a sign of hostility.
2. African Americans, especially men, do not like to share close spatial proximity, as this is a sign of aggression.
3. Negative suggestions (verbal or non-verbal) about their mothers can evoke instant physical confrontation.
4. It is considered a sign of disrespect to refer to African Americans by their first name.
5. African Americans do not like shaking hands or being called "Brother" by non-African Americans trying to relate. Many indicate: "They won't even let us have a handshake without taking it."
6. The "You people" phrase is considered a form of degradation and disrespect.
7. "Nigger" is a dehumanizing term when used by non-African Americans.

Summary

As the only group involuntarily brought to America and enslaved for two centuries, African Americans have a history of being policed. Many, therefore, hold negative views of law enforcement officers. Even African American officers experience disfavor because, to African Americans, they symbolize the establishment's control. African Americans have been instrumental in not only helping to build America, but in developing and enforcing laws that have maintained social order while being sensitive to the needs of all.

As racial counting and categories for African Americans were delineated in the 1800s, we are now experiencing some of the same sentiments in the twenty-first century. The Association of Multiethnic Americans successfully sought to include categories such as multiracial/multiethnic/multicultural on government application forms and the census. Thus, the 2000 census included multiracial individuals as a separate category.

Key Concepts

Back to Africa Movement	Family disclosure
Black Power	One drop rule
Brown v. Board of Education	Passing
Civil Rights Act	*Plessy v. Ferguson*
Extended family	Spirituality

Questions for Discussion

1. Explain the concept of involuntary immigration, and discuss how it impacted former slaves.

2. Discuss factors germane to the tenacity of African Americans' struggle for freedom.

3. Identify differences between the ideologies of Booker T. Washington and W.E.B. DuBois. Why have both philosophies been needed?

4. Discuss the relationship between law enforcement and African Americans. Place the discussion in a historical context and consider how contemporary issues perpetuate or reduce stress.

5. What do you suppose the impact will be when African Americans are no longer the largest minority group? Discuss what strategies (police minority populations) might emerge as a result.

Suggested Readings

Asante, M. 1990. *Kemet, Afrocentricity and Knowledge.* Trenton, NJ: African World Press.

Morrison, T. 1992. Playing in the Dark: Whiteness and the Literary Imagination. Cambridge, MA: Harvard University Press.

<www.census.gov> (Minority Links). Provides information on social and economic characteristics of the African American population.

<www.heritage.org/research/crime/CDAOO-05.cfm>. Research based on young African males and their continuing high homicide victimization rates in urban communities.

<www.nationalcenter.org/brown.html>. *Brown v. Board of Education* case outline to include Chief Justice Warren's written opinion.

<www.publicagenda.org/issues/nation_divided.cfm?issue_type=race>. Posted by Public Agenda Online. A series of questions involving the African American community, racial profiling, and policing.

<http://victims.firn.edu/pcbc.nsf>. The National Network of Preventing Crime in the Black Community.

CHAPTER 7

HATE CRIMES AND TERRORIST ACTIVITY

Learning Objectives

1. Discuss terrorism in the U.S., and identify its significance for law enforcement.
2. Explain if America is more conducive to terrorist acts today than historically.
3. Discuss pros and cons of how the FBI handled the Freeman standoff.
4. Identify factors inherent to an atmosphere that breeds terrorism.
5. Discuss the Hate Crimes Statistics Act and its impact on law enforcement.

Historical Perspective

While the U.S. Constitution grants all Americans rights, are these rights defined by popular opinion rather than guaranteed with citizenship (Harris 1995)? As discussed in preceding chapters, the Supreme Court's interpretation of the Constitution is often influenced by the prevailing political atmosphere.

Such a phenomenon will likely persist in this democratic society. Prejudice, however, will also continue; people will not only voice their opinions, but some will act them out with violence. Hate crimes, classified as terrorism, have become frequent. Some researchers even speculate that the U.S. is living in a pressure cooker based on hate (Pinkney 1994). Most Americans, however, agree that every citizen is guaranteed freedom and assembly as outlined in the First Amendment, and no individuals or groups have the right to inflict violence on others because of sexual preference or racial/ethnic background.

The following are targets for terrorists or hate groups (Mullins 1988, 144):

1. U.S. Government. Violence is used to protest American policies. Primary targets are usually government facilities such as in the Oklahoma City bombing.
2. Corporations. U.S. corporations are targeted in South Africa, and abortion clinics are prime targets in the U.S.
3. Wealthy private citizens. Targeted for financial gain, or to force the government to change a policy.
4. Political organizations. Targeted to intimidate them into changing political views or making decisions differently.
5. Labor groups. Violence is used to persuade members to vote a certain way on a specific issue.
6. Minorities. Targeted to "cleanse" America.

This chapter will focus on the last category, minorities, that may incorporate elements of one or more of the other categories. While this book focuses on policing in a diverse society, it is necessary to discuss hate crimes to identify any historical legacies. It is anticipated that criminal justice students consider how hate groups impact law enforcement.

Ku Klux Klan (KKK)

The KKK is one of the oldest formal right wing organizations in America, and one of the first terrorist groups (Southern Poverty Law Center n.d.). The organization emerged in 1865 in Pulaski, Tennessee, the brainchild of six ex-confederate soldiers. In the aftermath of the Civil War, when many were unemployed, people sought to regain control of an increasingly mundane existence (Newton 2001). The six founders, most of whom had college education, modeled the KKK in the tradition of Greek fraternities—they modified a Greek name, adopted a constitution, and swore members to secrecy (Chalmers 1965, 9). Ku Klux Klan is a derivative of "Kuklos," which is Greek for "circle" (Sims 1996).

Accounts of the KKK's beginning vary. Some believe that the six men started the organization to have what they termed "fun," while others blame their frustration over having lost the Civil War. Either way, the Klan decided to prey upon slaves' superstitions by using white bed sheets to appear apparition-like, and by adopting frightening names like dragons, giants, and ghouls (Newton 2001). Klan members were deputized and used for night patrols to enforce slave curfews (Southern Poverty Law Center n.d.). Soon, the Klan resorted to beatings, lynchings, and castrations to keep African Americans in line.

The Klan appealed to many whites; not only did the organization aim to protect the white social order, but members wore hooded masks to conceal their identity. Whites joined the organization for a number of reasons: farmers sought revenge on African Americans for war reparations, past slave owners feared retaliation, and poor whites feared competition for jobs.

While the Klan's "boyish pranks" have not been characterized as violent by some historians (Chalmers 1965), they were. Like other hate groups, the Klan trained its members (including children) in a paramilitary fashion. Klan activities (burning crosses, bombings, lynchings, rapes, and murders of women and children) were designed to instill fear (Sims 1996).

General Nathan Bedford Forrest, the KKK's first Imperial Wizard and leader, claimed that white insecurity caused the organization to grow (Newton 2001). Under his leadership, not only were there attacks on blacks, but also on the Republican Party whom the Klan viewed as responsible for the emancipation of slaves (Newton 2001). General Forrest established new chapters, or "dens," all across the South (Newton 2001).

The Klan has three major organizational branches: the Invisible Empire, headquartered in Denham Springs, Louisiana, the Knights of the Klan in Metaire, Louisiana and Tuscumbia, Alabama, and the United Klans of America (UKA), headquartered in Tuscaloosa, Alabama. Smaller offshoots are also located throughout America (Mullins 1988).

After Reconstruction, Klan activity subsided. In Georgia in 1915, however, the organization reemerged, called the rising of the second Klan (Newton 2001). Under the leadership of Imperial Wizard William Simmons, membership polls increased, and members' socioeconomic status changed from farmers and poor white trash to openly political middle and upper-middle class whites. David Duke, for example, held a state congressional seat in Louisiana and ran for Governor. Recently, members have begun wearing military-style clothing such as boots and fatigues. In many southern states, Klan sympathizers are identified by the confederate flags waving from their trucks or homes.

The Aryan Nations
(a.k.a. Church of Jesus Christ Christian)

The Aryan Nations is considered the largest militant, right-wing organization in America (Mullins 1988). Founded in the late 1970s by Richard Butler in Hayden Lake, Idaho, its primary objective is the elimination of minority races, specifically Jews. Other objectives include developing a white homeland in specific states (Washington, Oregon, Idaho, Montana, and Wyoming) until the cleansing (elimination) process is completed, and promoting physical violence (Mullins 1988). Oaths are sworn to kill police officers, especially those who arrest members.

The Aryan Brotherhood, a component of the Aryan Nations, is prevalent in prisons as incarcerated whites organize for protection and self-preservation. Further, Tom Metzger, an ex-Klansman strategist, organized a skinhead organization called the Aryan Youth, and recruited thousands of young people. Metzger capitalized on telecommunications to relay his message—printed literature, videotapes, the Internet, bulletin boards, and telephone "hate" hot lines (Hamm 1993). Further, Metzger appeared on television shows such as Oprah and Geraldo.

FBI reports reveal that the skinheads, a neo-nazi group, are primarily composed of white males, but also some women. Their roles, however, are unequal, as the organization's philosophy is one of white male dominance. The female role seems to be one of educating and maintaining group order.

Members advance in the hierarchy by killing law enforcement officers (especially FBI agents), judges, and local politicians. Points are awarded based on who they kill. Even the U.S. President is a named target (Mullins 1988). While this may appear to contradict their goal of eliminating minorities, prominent officials are targets because they think differently to white supremacists.

As with similar hate groups whose members keep their information private, it is difficult to estimate the size of the Aryan Nations. Speculation has it that most of the membership is located in California, Texas, and Arizona. The Aryan Brotherhood, reportedly, is funded through illegal activities such as drugs, gambling, and extortion (Mullins 1988).

Skinheads

According to the FBI, the skinheads have been one of the most active domestic terrorist groups (Centre for National Security Studies 2004). Clark Reid Martell organized the first American neo-Nazi skinhead group in 1984 (Hamm 1993). Many American skinheads do not know how their organization began. Ironically, the original British skinheads built the model for their group by combining the cultures of black Jamaican immigrants (the cool "bad boys") with that of the white working class. The original British skinheads, therefore, assumed the task of keeping their community clear of undesirables, usually by violent means (street fighting and gang-type activity) (Hamm 1993). Although the FBI downplays the threat by suggesting that the skinheads lack national reach, the organization should not be taken lightly; members are still very much active in European countries.

Skinheads are young (between twelve and twenty-five years old) middle to upper class whites who are sympathetic to, and influenced by, Hitler's doctrines. Their philosophy is one of white supremacy, including anti-minority and anti-Jewish sentiment. They are willing to kill and be killed to preserve the white race. Typically, their heads are shaven, they wear jeans, boots, white T-shirts, leather jackets, and swastika emblems, and get pumped up to rock and heavy metal music (especially white supremacist groups such as "Screwdriver," "Skull head," and "No Remorse") (Hamm 1993). Young recruits are subjected to initiation rites similar to those of street gangs.

Some researchers attribute skinheads' development and perpetuation to the Reagan Administration. Because President Reagan did not do enough for the white working class in the 1980s, they claim, children became skinheads in response to their families' frustrations (Hamm 1993, 6).

Black Power Separatists

Like many white power separatists groups, black power separatists want to create separate states/territories for African Americans and, in some instances, people of color.

Nation of Islam

The oldest and most famous of such organizations is the Nation of Islam (which means nation of peace), also known as the Black Muslims. The organization was developed in 1930 by Wallace D. Fard Muhammad, considered by members to be God's incarnation on Earth (McCartney 1992). His mission was to resurrect the lost people of the Tribe of Shabazz from the lost nation of Asia, who by accounts were of African heritage. He converted Elijah Poole to the Islamic faith, changed his name to Elijah Muhammad (Fard believed that Euro names destroyed blacks' heritage), and made him the only true apostle of Allah (McCartney 1992, 167). Elijah Poole, a native of Detroit, Michigan, was said to be the divine representative who would bring truth and light to his lost people. Fard disappeared in 1934 and Elijah Muhammad, with only a fourth grade education, became the new leader.

Elijah Muhammad advocated black power, self-determination, and self-definition. Further, he professed tenets now shared by all black separatist groups:

1. The goal is separation, not integration;
2. Black people must determine their own lives and futures;
3. A separate homeland should not be in Africa, as African slaves built America; and
4. Blacks all over the world must unite.

Elijah Muhammad died in 1975, passing his leadership to his son, Wallace Muhammad. Muhammad moved the organization toward a more assimilative approach, encouraging Muslims to register for the army and participate in political activities—compromises that created internal friction and led to a split between Muhammad and a young rising upstart, Louis Farrakhan.

Farrakhan was a controversial figure—while he drove the October 16, 1995 Million Man March on Washington in which thousands of African American men demonstrated unity without any anticipated violence, he was considered dangerous because of his contacts in the Middle East and for his "un-American rhetoric." Additionally, Jewish people have criticized what they consider his anti-Semitic behavior.

Many consider Malcolm X the greatest Black Muslim of the twentieth century. Speculation exists that he was assassinated in 1965 because of his ability to mobilize and control thousands of people, including those of other faiths. To be sure, Malcolm X rebuilt a declining Nation of Islam into a nation of well-disciplined followers (McCartney 1992). Muslims, non-Muslims, people of color, and whites often quote his famous statement, "By any means necessary." While his assassin's identity remains uncertain, speculation exists among African Americans that the FBI and CIA were involved. Some have even claim that Louis Farrakhan was involved out of jealousy, to win control of the organization.

The Nation of Islam philosophy is centered on the belief that the races should be separate. Blacks are the chosen race, and while long oppressed, they will eventually conquer the "white devils" (McCartney 1992). The organization's red flag, depicting the sun, moon, and stars, represents universal peace and harmony. Members seek sanctuary from evil outside influences in temple. Traditionally, the religion has taught the need for cleanliness, both inward and outward. Inward cleanliness entails avoiding the ingestion of harmful substances such as alcohol, illegal drugs, tobacco, and pork. Outward cleanliness requires that men wear suits and ties, and women cover their bodies so that only the face is visible. In temple, women are separated from men and taught that family is the focal point of life.

Black Panther Party

Not all black power advocates desired separatism. In 1966, the Black Panther Party, headed by Bobby Seal and Minister of Defense Huey Newton, advocated learning self-defense to improve and distinguish African American communities (Pearson 1994, 139), and supported black/white cooperation. Newton, who had read the works of Plato, Fanon, and Mao Tse-tung, believed in the unity of African Americans. Education and organization, he professed, would move them to a point of self-determinism.

Militia Groups

According to *Covert Action Quarterly* (1995), the KKK and the neo-Nazis were the forerunners to the militia groups currently spreading through America. Militia groups have increased their activities over the last twenty years, triggering several armed conflicts and gaining the attention of federal law enforcement. Described as loosely affiliated groups united chiefly in their anti-government sentiment, many are composed of older ex-military personnel who believe that the government intervenes too much in citizens' lives. Government power, they believe, panders to immigrants, people of color, women, and environmentalists. Central anti-government concerns focus on issues such as gun control, taxes, constitutional liberties, and federal regulations (Berlet 1995).

Paramilitary or militia groups now exist, and are active in, over forty states, especially in the rural Pacific Northwest, intermountain West, Southwest, and pockets of New Hampshire, Pennsylvania, and Florida. These groups are dangerous primarily because of their military backgrounds. They threaten the democratic process by promoting patriotic emotionalism, creating an atmosphere that leads to increased governmental intervention as politicians push new laws through Congress without considering constitutional protections, and by providing media attention that wins public sentiment and recruits increasing numbers.

While their actions are not necessarily racially or ethnically motivated, they target government officials on an "enemy" list. According to the Institute for First Amendment Studies, a non-profit organization for education and research founded in 1984 to investigate groups posing a threat to First Amendment freedoms, this list was topped by former Attorney General Janet Reno, former FBI Director Louis Freeh, and other federal judges and members of Congress.

In the last ten years, three events have highlighted the rise of militia groups in American society: the Ruby Ridge situation, the Waco incident, and the Freeman standoff.

Ruby Ridge Situation

The events that took place at the Ruby Ridge compound, located in Boundary County, Idaho, substantiated separatist claims that the government is too involved in private affairs, increasingly using the military to enforce policy. Randy Weaver, who had attended several Aryan Nations meetings, was involved in an eleven-day standoff with the FBI that ended in the deaths of his wife, son, and a federal marshal. Former Green Beret Lieutenant Colonel James "Bo" Gritz, now considered a mentor in militia culture, persuaded Weaver to surrender. This situation led to the formation of numerous other militia groups such as John Trochman's Militia of Montana (MOM), and Gritz' Specially Prepared Individuals for Key Events (SPIKE).

Waco Incident

On February 28, 1993, at the Branch Davidian complex in Waco, Texas, the Alcohol, Tobacco & Firearms (ATF) and FBI tried to arrest David Koresh, militant leader of a religious cult, for firearm violations (Maas 1996). By the end of a prolonged standoff, ten people (including four ATF agents) died, and John Magaw became the newly-appointed director of the ATF.

Controversy continues to this day, as Congress investigated the government for their role in the incident. Many claimed that federal agencies were out of control and needed reorganization. Some congressional representatives called for the abolishment of the ATF, or the merging of the ATF with other federal law enforcement organizations (Maas 1996). Under the current leadership of Attorney General John Ashcroft, these law enforcement organizations are undergoing major reorganizations—consideration has been given to combining federal agencies (e.g., ATF and FBI) and bringing on new organizational heads (Office of Homeland Security).

Freeman Standoff

On March 25, 1996, Leroy Schweitzer and Daniel Petersen, Jr., two leaders of the Montana Freemen, were arrested in an FBI sting operation. The eighty-one-day standoff occurred on a 960-acre farm where twenty Freemen were surrounded by approximately one hundred FBI agents. The standoff began when the Freemen's patriarch, Ralph Clark, refused to leave the farm (Knapp 1996). Many of the Freemen held in the compound were under federal and state indictment on charges ranging from bad checks to threatening to kidnap and kill a federal judge.

The FBI did allow two top negotiators to meet with the Freemen—former policeman Jack McLamb, and former Green Beret Lieutenant Colonel James Gritz. Gritz, credited with Randy Weaver's surrender during the Ruby Ridge situation, stated that the Freemen wore guns strapped to their bodies and kept guns in every room. According to Gritz, they were anti-government; they believed that they were not subject to federal or state laws, but were sovereign citizens of their own country, governed only by common law (CNN 1996).

Law Enforcement Encounters with Hate and Terrorists Groups

Hate groups present a great deal of frustration for state, local, and federal agents. Often, the nature of their activity dictates that law enforcement take the lead in the investigation; territorial issues must often be resolved before a criminal investigation can even begin. In cases focused on minority hates crimes, for example, it must be determined whether the FBI will receive assistance from state and local police when investigating crimes involving civil rights violations (e.g., church bombings and lynchings). Local agents feel intimidated by federal agents who, they believe, perceive them as incompetent.

Hate crimes involve many people or organizational sanctions. Even though one or two individuals commit the act, there may be organizational support; trying to stop the organization is often slow and frustrating.

Finally, police often become a target for hate groups. The situation, therefore, becomes more emotional, hindering the investigation.

Domestic Terrorism

Domestic terrorism, as broadly defined in the USA Patriot Act, refers to "acts dangerous to human life that are a violation of criminal laws of the U.S. or of any state" (USA Patriot Act 2001). This includes attempts to intimidate or coerce a civilian population, or to influence government policy by mass destruction, assassination, or kidnapping. This broad definition allows for discretion by law enforcement officers as they protect the homeland.

The Department of Homeland Security (DHS) is responsible for protecting communities and private citizens. U.S. Secretary of Homeland Security Tom Ridge has initiated a number of initiatives to combat domestic terrorism, ranging from safe school initiatives to cyber and mail initiatives. In addition, the DHS is responsible for securing domestic travel—an enormous task that involves the screening of not only commercial air planes, but busses and trains.

A Homeland Security Advisory system is in place that informs Americans daily (on television and the Internet) of the security threat levels:

- Red. Most severe. Government and public facilities may close, and specialized units may be mobilized.
- Orange. High. Precautionary actions are taken (e.g., public events are monitored).
- Yellow. Elevated. Increased surveillance of critical areas and landmarks.
- Blue. Guarded. Emergency procedures are updated, and the public is kept aware of terrorist potential.
- Green. Lowest. Provides training, assessments of vulnerabilities, and monitoring.

Pinkney (1994) suggests that America is no longer a melting pot or mosaic, but more like a pressure cooker. As society becomes more diverse and technology connects the world, it is anticipated that people will become more stressed and less tolerant. They will feel increasingly threatened and competitive in education and the job market.

Law enforcement organizations, too, will feel the pressure as they are often directly or indirectly involved in problematic situations. For example, some may become involved in controlling or responding to acts of terrorism in order to protect the homeland—at which time they are faced with the task of enforcing the laws while simultaneously protecting citizens. As officers perform their duties as prescribed by law, especially during this time of terrorist alertness, they face a difficult responsibility—they must be alert and aggressive, while also being mindful to safeguard constitutional rights.

Federal agencies continue to be ridiculed by citizens and militia groups. Some congressional members have stereotyped them as "Jack-booted government thugs" (Maas 1996, 6). Law enforcement organizations must endure the same prejudice and discrimination faced by many minorities and ethnic groups. Landau's (1995) prediction that America might become a land of angry people without a Constitution seems inevitable.

Even civilians cannot escape terrorism. Bombings are relatively new to America. Major attacks have recently occurred: the World Trade Center, Oklahoma City, and, the most devastating, the 9/11 attacks on the World Trade Center and the Pentagon.

The World Trade Center (1993)

Mohammed Salameh was accused of bombing the World Trade Center on February 26, 1993. He used a rented van carrying large amounts of explosives. Six people died and more than a thousand were injured (Maas 1996). Much speculation has surrounded this incident, as Salameh's accomplice, Emid Ali Salem, claimed that he warned the FBI but they did nothing.

Oklahoma City Bombing

At 9:02 a.m. on April 19, 1995, the Albert P. Murrah Federal building in Oklahoma City was bombed. There were over four hundred causalities, leaving 168 dead (including fifteen children). Desert Storm veteran Timothy McVeigh was arrested, claiming the bombings to be revenge for both Ruby Ridge and Waco. McVeigh was taken into custody and charged with mass destruction to kill and injure innocent people as well as destruction of federal property. His trial started April 24, 1997. On June 13, 1997, he was sentenced by the jury to die, and was executed by lethal injection at 7:14 a.m. on June 11, 2001.

9/11

Prior to September 11, 2001, a number of hate crimes and/or terrorist attacks against the U.S. occurred on foreign soil (e.g., USS Cole, U.S. Embassies in Kenya and Tanzania, bombing U.S. soldiers in Saudi Arabia)—all of which contributed to the U.S. declaring war on Iraq. The 9/11 attacks on the World Trade Center and the Pentagon, however, lit the fuse. The 9/11 terrorist acts have left law enforcement in a real dilemma. Forty-five days after the attack, for example, Congress passed the USA Patriot Act without debate—the intent of which being to reduce terrorism and punish those committing the acts as well as those aiding terrorists. Additionally, the act aimed to enhance law enforcement officers' investigatory powers. Organizations such as the American Civil Liberties Union (ACLU), however, argue that the act, allowing officers access to private records (e.g., medical, education) without a warrant, probable cause, and without having to inform the suspect, infringes on citizens' rights and liberties. Even under the scrutiny of the ACLU and other "watch" organizations, some congressional leaders see the need to pass Patriot

II, an act that would give officers even more power (e.g., wiretapping, detention, and prosecution).

Summary

America has endured many domestic and foreign terrorist acts. Individual differences and the right to peacefully express ideas without fear of punishment are values that make America unique. Individuals, however, must continue to monitor, discuss, and participate in the implementation of laws, procedures, and policies.

The U.S. Government is now faced with a different type of enemy—individuals motivated by religious mysticism, who believe that self-sacrifice will earn them a better life after death. As hate crimes and foreign and domestic terrorism are becoming seemingly commonplace on American soil, there is a desperate need to rely on law enforcement; incidents like Ruby Ridge and Waco, however, have instilled fear and distrust in many citizens. To protect America, more laws will likely be enacted extending the powers of law enforcement against terrorists. As new strategies emerge to fight terrorism, what rights will Americans be asked to sacrifice?

Key Concepts

Aryan Nation	Neo-Nazis
Black Panther Party	Ruby Ridge
Hate Crime	Standoff
KKK	Statistics Act
Montana Freemen	Waco Incident
Nation of Islam	World Trade Center Bombing

Questions for Discussion

1. What are some concerns with the definition of terrorism?
2. Has the twenty-first century experienced a different type of terrorism/terrorist? Explain.
3. How has American changed since 9/11 in terms of homeland security?

4. Identify factors germane to acts of domestic terrorism.
5. Discuss some of the dilemmas facing law enforcement officers responsible for homeland security.

Suggested Reading

<www.dhs.gov>. Department of Homeland Security.

<http://dp.sbccom.army.mil>. Domestic Preparedness homepage.

<www.fbi.gov/page2/nov03/hcs111203.htm>. Hate crime statistics published from 1999 to 2002.

<www.kkk.com>. The official website of the Ku Klux Klan and their mission.

<www.ojp.usdoj.gov/archive/topics/hate/technical_assistance.htm>. Posted by the Office of Justice Programs, this page offers technical training for law enforcement agencies in recognizing and dealing with hate crimes and terrorist acts.

<www.whitehouse.gov/news/releases/2001/01/print/20011008.html>. Information about the establishment of the Office of Homeland Security.

CHAPTER 8

HISPANICS AND POLICING

Learning Objectives

1. Discuss why the Hispanic population is considered an in-between minority.
2. Explain the factors that led to different waves of Hispanics entering America.
3. Explain how Hispanics are stereotyped. What effect does this have?
4. Explain Proposition 187.
5. Discuss interactions between police and Hispanics.

Historical Perspective

When the Spanish first set foot in the Americas alongside early explorers like Americus Vespucci and Ponce de Leon, they were referred to as Spaniards or Spanish. As different people of Spanish origin began to enter America, the white population coined the term Hispanic (meaning old time home in Spain) (Cafferty & Engstrom 2000).

Today, the terms Hispanic and Latino are used interchangeably. It was not until the 1970 census that specific questions were asked about Hispanic origin, and Latino only just appeared on the 2000 census (Guzman 2001). People of Spanish ancestry dislike the term Hispanic, as they consider it Eurocentric—they prefer Latino (Marger 1994). The term Hispanic is used throughout this chapter not out of disrespect, but because it seems the preferred terminology in this part of the country.

Hispanics are descendants of the Moors of Africa who invaded Spain in the eighth century B.C; it took the Spanish underground over seven hundred years to drive the Moors back out. The Moors, however, left behind beautiful and unique art and architecture (The New Book of Knowledge 1984) and many hues of people of African descent (Bigler 2003). Takaki (1993) discusses the impact of the genetic link between the Spanish and the Moors, using terms such as "mongrelized people" (Bigler 2003, 211).

Hispanics entered America in many different ways—as explorers, leading crews to the continent, immigrating, or illegally. Today, they continue to come—some seeking gainful economic opportunities, some escaping political turmoil and/or persecution at home, and all searching for a better life. Indeed, the U.S. has become the fifth largest Spanish- speaking country (Gonzalez 2000, 207). Primarily composed of Cubans, Mexicans, Puerto Ricans, and South and Central Americans, the Hispanic population is expected to be America's largest minority group by 2010.

In-Between Minority

Hispanics have been described as an in-between minority because, unlike other groups, they have not experienced the psychological trauma of genocide, slavery, or relocation. Weyr (1988) suggests that Hispanics are "cultural relativists," caught between cultures and wanting the best of both worlds. They are rejected by society because of their heritage (especially if they retain their mother tongue), yet are to some degree accepted if they assimilate.

Hispanics also experience this in-between status racially, as their physical appearance is a combination of African and other nationalities. Some look African American, while others look Anglo American. This creates conflict not only in society, but within families, as children whose African heritage is more dominant may receive more negative reinforcement than those with dominant Euro heritage.

Hispanics are caught between two warring cultures—they struggle to retain their heritage (although at the same time seem embarrassed of their Moorish ancestors), while also trying to look and act Anglo in order to assimilate into mainstream society. Weyr (1988) describes those who assimilate well as lacking Hispanicity. The near-white or white Hispanic experiences an easier transition into society than does an Asian, African American, or black Hispanic.

Hispanic Hierarchy

Hispanics, making up 12.5 percent (35.3 million) of the population, are extremely heterogeneous (Guzman 2001). They are categorized by ethnicity—

Cubans, Mexicans, Puerto Ricans, or Central and South Americans. It is important to understand the differences between the groups.

Cubans

Cubans are considered the most prosperous Hispanic group because they are, for the most part, better educated. Comprising 0.4 percent of the population, they live mainly in Florida, but have also migrated throughout the country (Guzman 2001). Miami, their primary entrance point into the U.S., is known as Little Havana. Florida is a bilingual state, with Spanish the second language.

Cubans entered the U.S. in three waves: 1959-65 (middle and upper class professionals, and business people), 1965-73 (working and lower class), and 1980-82 (the boatlift people, mainly criminals, mentally ill, and those considered a threat to Cuba's government). This group comprised the largest number of immigrants (Shusta et al. 1995).

Cubans, especially those with a Euro appearance, prosper because they understand the capitalistic work ethic. They own more businesses than other Hispanic groups (e.g., Mexicans), and use their purchasing power.

Cubans tend to isolate themselves from other Hispanics, initially because they thought they would return to Cuba when Castro fell. As many have lived in the U.S. for over twenty years, however, it is doubtful that they would now choose to return.

Mexicans

Mexicans are the largest Hispanic group with 7.3 percent of the U.S. population and 58.5 percent of the Hispanic population (Guzman 2001). They are primarily concentrated in Southwestern states such as Southern California, Texas, and Arizona. Most came in search for jobs (Cafferty & Engstrom 2000); indeed, Mexicans tend to be migrant farmers who work long hours for little pay. Many males, who left their families in Mexico, are considered transient because they move back and forth between families and jobs. Most work in factories and gas stations—while jobs with the city and state government would enable them to send more money to home to their families, such work is often closed to Mexicans as many are illegal, undereducated, or unable to speak English.

The media negatively stereotypes the Mexican American, portraying them as lazy, indifferent, or drunk.

Puerto Ricans

At 1.2 percent of the American population (Guzman 2001), Puerto Ricans have a different status than other Hispanics because they are American citizens. Residing primarily in the Northeast (e.g., New York and New Jersey), they are less affluent than other Hispanics (Cafferty & Engstrom 2000) and, as depicted in the movie "West Side Story," are stereotyped as excitable and macho, or gang bangers, lovers, and switchblade carriers.

Central and South Americans

Central and South Americans, at 3.6 percent of the population, represent the "other" Hispanic category in the 2000 census (Guzman 2001). Most have migrated from locations such as Columbia, Nicaragua, and El Salvador, escaping political turmoil and drug wars.

This group has gone unnoticed until recent Senate hearings. Many prominent Americans employ Central and South Americans without filing federal income tax statements—these employees, therefore, are either illegal or wrongfully claim Puerto Rican ancestry (Cafferty & Engstrom 2001). The Simpson-Rodino Act of 1986 stipulated that illegal immigrants could no longer be employed, and legalized those immigrants whose sponsors supported them as industrious workers (Gonzalez 2000).

More recently, concern has arisen over the use of vulnerable Central and South American children as cheap labor. The media has seized on this issue since it was found that Kathy Lee Gifford and Michael Jordan had invested in businesses allegedly using child labor.

Family Values

Historically, the Hispanic man has been the dominant decision-maker in the family, the woman the primary care provider with little input into household decisions. As Hispanic women enter the job market, however, this trend is changing. But as women go to work, they are faced with finding a Spanish-speaking childcare to ensure that the children retain their mother tongue. Moreover, husbands of working women tend to experience a sense of powerlessness that results in marital strife and often leads to their using escape mechanisms such as alcoholism and drug use (Shapiro 1998).

Though their roots may differ, Hispanic families share similar value systems and customs. Over fifty percent of the Hispanic population belongs to the

Catholic Church. Other religious organizations are vying for Hispanic support, luring them into churches by making services more colorful and emotional.

Political Involvement

The African American experience has had a great impact on Hispanics. The Chicano Movement (1965-75), also called the Brown Power Movement, was named after the Black Power Movement of the 1960s and 1970s (Morales 2002). Many Hispanic leaders arose from this movement. Cesare Chavez, a Mexican American, fought for social justice by uniting farm workers and calling national attention to the exploitation of Mexican American grape pickers. Chavez started the union—the Farm Workers Association (FWA), later known as the United Farm Workers (UFW), was founded in Fresno, California, in 1962. Because Chavez focused on the family unit, women played an important role; indeed, Delores Huerta is often considered its co-founder (Gonzales 1999).

In 1966, the FWA and the Filipino Agricultural Workers Organizing Committee merged to form the United Farm Workers Organizing Committee (UFWOC). To fight for higher pay and human rights for farmers, Chavez organized a boycott of non-union grape pickers that lasted from 1968-70. His protests were non-violent (sit-ins, marches, and fasting), modeled after Gandhi and King Jr., and resulted in bringing about much needed reform in health care, pensions, and unemployment benefits (Gonzales 1999). Chavez became not only a nationally renowned non-violent leader, but a Chicano icon (Morales 2002). When he died in 1993, over forty thousand attended his funeral in Delano, California. California established a state holiday for him in 2000, and in 2003, the U.S. Post Office issued the Chavez commemorative stamp (Gonzales 1999).

Reyes Tijerina also became a leader. More militant, he sought the return of all the land that had been taken from Spanish people (Morales 2002), advocating violent means if necessary. In 1963, he founded the Alianza Federation de Mercedes (Federation Alliance of land grants) in New Mexico, aiming to gain compensation for families whose land had been taken from them by the U.S. Government. In 1965, Rodolfo Gonzales founded the Crusade for Justice to provide Mexican Americans with social services and job opportunities. In 1970, Jose Angel Gutierrez helped organize La Raza Unida, a Texas political party with the primary goal to register Mexican Americans. Still, many Hispanics did not vote because they felt that their vote would make no difference.

Thus, while political influence has not increased at the same rate as the Hispanic population, the group has still made great gains politically. Not only did they learn to use non-violent protest, but they became politically astute. By the end of the 1960s, Hispanics began applying for federal jobs and establishing their own lobbyists. Four Hispanics held seats in the House of Representatives (Wyre 1988): Joseph Montoya of New Mexico, Eligio de La Garza and Henry Gonzalez of Texas, and Edward R. Roybal of California. Since the 1970s, numerous others have held high political office: Vicente Ximenes was chairman of the cabinet committee on Mexican American Affairs and U. S. Commissioner of the Equal Employment Opportunity Commission (the first Mexican American to be so named) in 1967; Hector Garcia became a member of the U.S. delegation to the UN in 1967; and Raul H. Castro was appointed U.S. Ambassador to El Salvador from 1964-68. He also became the first Mexican American Governor of Arizona in 1974. There are over twenty Hispanic congressmen and women, many elected to local and state offices, and still more presidential appointments.

Several organizations also emerged, escalating the Hispanic cause in the political arena. In 1976, the Hispanic Congressional Caucus developed to provide Congressional representatives of Latin origin a forum in which to discuss issues, strategize on how to make their votes count, and consider current events. The Mexican American Political Association (founded in 1960) and the League of United Latin American Citizens (LULAC) (founded in 1929 in conjunction with community support as Chavez did with the UFW) (Gonzalez 2000) also emerged to advance the economic, educational, and political conditions for Hispanics.

The Hispanic population is one of the youngest (median age twenty-three) and fastest growing minority groups. As it continues to grow, politicians will undoubtedly pay the group increased attention. Recent concentration has been focused on how to control the number of illegal immigrants reported to be entering the U.S. via the California border. Some states have sought control through legislation. In California in 1994, Governor Peter Wilson passed Proposition 187 (also called the "Save Our State" initiative because its primary purpose was to stop illegal immigration). Others suggested the use of military force to control the number of illegal immigrants. Few, however, agreed—military force, they said, was best used in foreign countries or to help Americans during domestic disasters such as tornados and fires. The passage of Proposition 187 set off major debate as it not only denied social services, health care, and education to families of illegal immigrants, but its suspicion clause required local law enforcement officers and teachers to report everyone suspected of being illegal.

Hispanics tried to repeal the measure on the grounds that the suspicion clause would lead to or perpetuate discrimination, and that children should not be made to suffer for their parents' decisions. The American Civil Liberties Union (ACLU), along with four other civil rights organizations, filed to repeal 187 on the basis that it violated the Fourteenth Amendment's due process clause (taking away rights without a hearing), citing *Plyler v. Doe* (1982) in which the Supreme Court struck down a Texas statute denying undocumented children public education as a violation of the Fourteenth Amendment's equal protection clause (Mailman 1995). On March 19, 1998, Proposition 187 was ruled unconstitutional.

California voters, however, remained passionate about the initiative; it returned as a focal point in California's 2003 gubernatorial elections as Governor Gray Davis, a Democrat, was recalled with a special election and lost his seat to Arnold Schwarzenegger, who had voted for Proposition 187 in 1994.

Spanish vs. English

While Hispanics have a longer history in America than other minorities (except Native Americans), they are considered foreigners because they speak a different language. While an important part of ancestral heritage, many third or fourth generation immigrants have given up their mother tongue. Hispanics, for the most part, aim to be bilingual. They question school systems that suggest children speak only English, demanding instead that schools hire Spanish-speaking teachers and teach Spanish as a second language. Increasing numbers of schools are stressing the need for Spanish, and many law enforcement organizations are recruiting Spanish-speaking officers. Emerging bilingual programs, however, are criticized for slowing the assimilation process and encouraging separatism (Cafferty & Engstrom 2000).

In California, where Hispanics make up a majority of the population, they question minimum standards for jury selection (28 U.S.C. § 1865(b) (1968)), contending that a jury without Hispanics is not a jury of their peers. Critics respond, however, that all jury members must meet minimum standards, one of which being that they read, write, and speak English.

Stereotypes

The Hispanic population is not homogeneous. The following stereotypes, however, consider it so:

1. Some police officers consider Hispanics foreigners, without care to their ancestry. Some comment that they should go back to Mexico when, in fact, they are of Cuban heritage.

2. Some officers believe that young Hispanics with low riding cars are either gang members or school dropouts. While many do ride around in groups, this does not imply gang affiliation.
3. Lazy. This stereotype has developed out of a misunderstanding of Hispanics' laidback demeanor.
4. Many officers presume that Hispanics can only speak Spanish. When arriving on a scene, therefore, they might address comments to whichever person is able to speak English.

Police and Hispanic Interactions

According to Cafferty & Engstrom (2000), Hispanics and police have a negative relationship, in part because of how Hispanics interacted with police in their countries of origin. In Mexico and South and Central America, for example, police accept bribes and abuse their power. Few citizens speak out against them, however, because they are powerful. Often, government officials even sanction their abusive behavior. Although some American police officers behave the same way, the checks and balances system prevents such blatant abuses of power. Because America is a democracy, it is thought that the powers invested in police officers flow from and through the people. The people, therefore, can move to provide police sanctions (civilian review boards). Still, many Hispanics, fearing police corruption, stereotype the "cop on the take."

Negative feelings are also the result of two major incidents. In 1942, nine Mexican American youths were convicted of murder and spent two years in San Quentin prison. After careful consideration of the evidence, a Los Angeles appellate court overturned the conviction (Dinnerstein et al. 1990, 251). Many Mexican Americans, however, hold this situation up as an example of justice for Hispanics. In the 1943 Zoot Suit Riots, sailors in Los Angeles beat Mexican Americans for acting defiant and unpatriotic in wearing oversized suits (because of war time rations, the suits were considered a luxury item) (Morales 2002).

More recently, a situation occurred in Los Angeles paralleling the Rodney King incident. Two state troopers chased and stopped a truck carrying twenty illegal Mexicans. Many escaped; two, however, were severely beaten. Because the incident was videotaped by a news helicopter team, America witnessed the beating and voiced their concern.

There are many explanations for the friction between Hispanics and police officers. First, the language barrier blocks understanding. Police officers, feeling that Hispanics should be able to speak English, become frustrated. Some even accuse Hispanics of pretending not to understand. Hispanics, in turn, become frustrated that the officer is unable to speak Spanish. Secondly, officers fail to understand that Hispanics view officers as corrupt because of previous negative experiences, and that their behavior evokes fear and anger. Finally, stereotyping plays a major role in the misunderstanding. Police organizations have tried to recruit, train, and retain Hispanic police officers; the gap between the number of Hispanic police officials and the size of the Hispanic population, however, remains wide.

Summary

The Hispanic population is the fastest growing segment in America. Even with a decline in birthrate (unlikely), Hispanics will continue to be the largest minority. The implications are great. Hispanics will have more political clout, which will mean more impact on political representatives in drafting and passing legislation.

Law enforcement is already feeling the Hispanic presence. Along with other strategies such as recruitment of Hispanics, criminal justice students are being encouraged to learn Spanish.

Key Concepts

Bilingual	Moors
Chavez	Mother tongue
Cubans	Proposition 187
Hispanicity	Puerto Ricans
In-Between Minority	Zoot Suit Riots

Questions for Discussion

1. Discuss the twenty-first century shift in minority populations, and the implications for law enforcement.

2. Discuss the pros and cons of Proposition 187.

3. Discuss why the Hispanic population is referred to as an in-between minority.

4. Explain the Hispanic hierarchy and describe traits of each level.

5. Hispanics have a long history of encounters with law enforcement. Discuss how such encounters played a significant role in the current stress that exists between the groups.

Suggested Reading

Alozie, N.O. 1999. Segregation of black and hispanic group outcomes: Policing in large cities. *American Politics Research,* 27(3), 354–375.

Nieto, S. 2000. Affirming Diversity: The Sociopolitical Context of Multicultural Education (3rd ed.). New York, NY: Addison Wesley Longman.

Oboler, S. 1995. *Ethnic Labels, Latino Lives: Identity and Politics of (Re)presentation in the United States.* Minneapolis, MN: University of Minnesota Press.

<www.hispanicprwire.com_NAAHP_ENG.htm>. This home page of the National Association for the Advancement of Hispanic People deals with their involvement in local and national community, policing, and politics.

<www.lib.niu.edu/ipo/im911209.html>. *Today's Policing within the Hispanic Community.*

<www.omhrc.gov/haa/HAA2pg/AboutHAAla.htm>. Website refers to major stereotypes about Hispanics in the United States.

CHAPTER 9

GAYS AND LESBIANS AND POLICE ENCOUNTERS

Learning Objectives

1. Discuss the Stonewall Riots and their significance to the Gay Liberation Movement.
2. Explain the factors that led to the Gay Rights Movement.
3. Explain how homophobic thinking can hinder police officers' performance.
4. Explain why some police officers have low tolerance in dealing with gays, lesbians, and bisexuals.
5. Discuss the prevalence of HIV among gays, lesbians, and bisexuals.

Historical Perspective

Homosexuality has existed since the beginning of civilization. Socrates, Aristotle, and Plato all wrote about their homosexual relationships, including those that existed among their Greek gods (e.g., Zeus, Hercules). Dover and Dover (1978) document overt homosexuality in everyday Greek society, as depicted in education, arts, literature, vocabulary, and legislation. Clearly, Greeks thought homosexuality normal; it was as widespread as heterosexuality, and considered important to the male maturation process (Adam 1995). Although young men often left their families to live with older men, they were still expected to marry and have a family after nineteen years of age—exclusive homosexuality was discouraged because it threatened the continuation of Greek civilization (Seidman 1996).

From the time of the Greeks to the rise of the Roman Catholic Church, public opinion shifted. Like the Greeks, the Romans accepted homosexuality.

Unlike the Greeks, however, they implemented stringent laws against homosexual practices—stringent not for any moral reason, but because rigid legal codes and discipline were commonplace. While homosexuality was not openly condoned, neither was it considered sinful or unnatural. Even after the fall of the Roman Empire, many of its laws impacted world civilizations. The Roman Catholic Church, for example, assimilated components of Roman laws into its doctrine, including those relating to homosexual behaviors.

Many organized Christian religions condemn homosexual practices. The flesh is a source of human weakness, they preach, and sexual intercourse ought to be practiced for procreation rather than pleasure (Seidman 1996). Homosexuality, therefore, was associated with paganism and further marginalized. The preeminent theologian Thomas Aquinas wrote extensively about the evils of homosexuality, classifying it as worse than rape or adultery.

Contemporary Christian attitudes differ. Blumenfeld & Raymond (1993) delineate three theological positions:

1. Those that blatantly condemn the practice (e.g., Catholic Church, Southern Baptist Convention).
2. Those that neither pass judgment nor accept (e.g., United Methodist Church, Lutheran Church). This group embraces the person but not the behavior, believing all sins should be forgiven, homosexuals are children of God, and the church must assist homosexuals in overcoming their condition.
3. Those that accept homosexuality as they would heterosexuality (e.g., Metropolitan Community Church, Friends, United Church of Christ). This group emphasizes love between all; nothing is bad in and of itself, *mala in se*. Church rituals are open to everyone, including homosexuals (Seidman 1996).

Definition of Terms

The terms "homosexual" and "gay and lesbian" will be used interchangeably throughout this chapter as they both imply same-sex behavior. Homosexual men adopted the term "gay" to counter such negative names as "fag," "homo," and "queer." The term is something of a political statement, exemplifying pride in who they are and what they represent (Cruikshank 1992).

"Lesbian," the female homosexual, comes from the Greek "Lesbos," an island in the Aegean Sea noted for its lyric poets and Sappho's reputed homosexuality. Lesbians have always been less visible than gays—or perhaps as visible, but interestingly, taken less seriously. While it was socially acceptable for women to hold hands in public, embrace, or kiss on the cheek, men were subject to scrutiny if they exhibited the same behavior. Just as different standards are used in determining "correct" male and female actions and roles, so they are used to separate lesbian from gay behavior (Seidman 1996).

Traditionally, men in America are characterized as strong, stable, and in control of their emotions. If they behave weak, unstable, or emotional, they are labeled effeminate and homosexual. Because women, as primary care providers, are encouraged to be caring, passionate, and sensitive, such characteristics are acceptable even when directed toward other women. It is also acceptable for women to wear men's clothing. In the corporate world, for example, a woman can gain power by "dressing for success." If a man wears women's clothing, however, he is labeled abnormal or deviant (Blumenfeld & Raymond 1993).

Today, the idea of "family" is no longer restricted by bloodlines, gender, or geographic proximity. Unlike the traditional model of two adults (woman and man) and two children (girl and boy), the 1990s definition broadened to include all adults (man and/or woman, of varying numbers) and children (biological or otherwise) living together and providing for each other emotionally, financially, and physically. Families traditionally "matriarchal" are now "single parent," and those traditionally "dysfunctional" are now "disorganized." "Dysfunctional" denotes the presence of a certain amount of pathology; moreover, it is unclear what constitutes a "functional" family, as all experience some abnormalities (based on societal definition).

Gays and lesbians define themselves, and their community, as family. The 1970s song "We Are Family" by Sister Sledge is considered the homosexual anthem (Case et al. 1995, 165). This notion of community as family is practiced in other cultures (e.g., African American, Asian), but it presents difficulty for many citizens and law enforcement officers when interacting with gays and lesbians because mainstream America keeps family separate from deviant homosexual behavior.

Coming Out

Gays and lesbians are a diverse minority, composed of many racial, ethnic, and religious groups. They may, in fact, be America's largest minority group; there is no way of knowing, however, because many do not disclose their homosexuality for fear of losing respect, a job, or family. Society accepts the notion of two men or two women living together, but some consider same-sex intercourse a violation of natural laws (to suppress homosexuality, many leg-islators have supported the passage of sodomy laws). Those who do "come out" (openly admit to being gay or lesbian) experience harassment, discrim-ination, and possible loss of family.

Like in other minority communities, gays and lesbians withhold some in-formation from outsiders. If a member wants to keep his sexual orientation quiet, for example, peers will generally respect his wishes. According to Cruik-shank (1992), this code of silence is changing. For several reasons, more younger gays and lesbians are "outing" (revealing someone's sexual orienta-tion) each other because they: 1) feel that closeted members are not true to themselves and create undue stress on themselves and their families, 2) fear the HIV/AIDS epidemic, and 3) believe that if more prominent citizens would come out of the closet, homophobic fears would be alleviated.

Coming out has created much debate and, at times, anger among gays and lesbians. Some consider outing a form of psychological violence that should not be inflicted on anyone (Cruikshank 1992, 170). On one hand, it is argued, Michelangelo's or Henry James' greatness should not have been overshadowed by sexual orientation; on the other, if they had made public their sexual ori-entation, they might never have attained such success.

While many gays and lesbians have come out and are trying to raise aware-ness about homosexuality, many others (especially athletes, movie stars, and politicians) remain closeted because they fear placing their lives and careers in jeopardy. This group, therefore, opts to provide alternative explanations for their activities. If some famous person is diagnosed as HIV positive, for ex-ample, their publicist is quick to claim a means of transmission other than homosexual activity.

Matrimony

In 2003, Massachusetts became the only state to allow gay couples to legally marry with the *Goodridge v. Department of Public Health* decision. The case originated as a class action lawsuit filed on behalf of seven same-sex couples who were denied marriage licenses. The constitutional issue was whether Massachusetts could deny the protections, benefits, and obligations of civil marriage to same-sex couples. The Court ruled that the licenses could not be denied because Massachusetts did not present any "constitutionally adequate reason," and issued an advisory opinion that gays are entitled to "nothing less than marriage." Further, the Court stated that, while their decision would be met with controversy, their "obligation is to define liberty of all not a mandate our own moral code." As of May 2004, therefore, gay couples could marry in Massachusetts (Peter 2004).

It remains unclear what impact this decision will have on the other thirty-eight states (as well as the federal government) that do not legally recognize gay marriage. Indeed, all eyes are on the state of matrimony between same-sex partners as legislators consider what could be the third landmark gay-liberation case. In *Lawrence v. Texas* (2003), the Supreme Court ruled that laws criminalizing gay sex violate civil rights. Some states are preparing for the possibility of a decision in favor of homosexual unions. North Carolina, for example, passed a bill declaring same-sex marriages performed in other states illegal (Daily Reflector 1996); it is likely that other states will follow suit. Because of the Supreme Court's 2003 ruling that individuals cannot be prosecuted for what they do in the privacy of their own bedrooms, however, gay and lesbian rights activists will surely try harder than ever to legalize such unions.

Children of Gay and Lesbian Couples

"Nature v. Nurture" is an age-old debate that questions whether homosexuality is a learned behavior or is the result of genetics. Regardless of the position taken, many would like to criminalize homosexual behavior; some states have moved in this direction with sodomy laws. When the courts place children, they consider whether or not a parent will expose the child to criminal behavior. Concerns exist that children of homosexuals will be subject to unnecessary psychological or physical abuse by society, or will become homosexual. If these concerns are valid, how is it that the majority of homosexuals were raised in heterosexual households? Society's primary concern should be the quality of care that children receive, not the sexual orientation of their parents.

American courts have based their decisions on what is best for the child, traditional values (moral judgment), whether homosexuality is a physiological condition or a learned behavior, and geographic area. Bible belt courts, for example, tend to take a more stringent position against gay or lesbian couples adopting children.

In divorce situations, the court most often names the mother as primary caretaker. If she has committed any "moral sins" such as lesbianism, however, the courts will consider placing the child with the straight father or an extended family member. Gay couples also experience difficulties with adoptions. Social service agencies, however, appear to be opting for gay or lesbian couples rather than allowing children to remain in state-operated facilities.

Stereotypes

Many police officers will tolerate people of a different race or ethnicity sooner than they will gays. Heterosexual police officers might refuse to work with a homosexual officer even though they worked well together and held mutual respect before his sexual orientation was revealed. These officers hold the same misconceptions as the general homophobic public, such as that gays and lesbians want to have sex with every man or woman they interact with. Homosexuals, however, are no different than heterosexuals; sexual attraction is based on many factors.

To be sure, homosexual stereotypes abound. Homosexual men are stereo-typically effeminate in action and appearance. Homosexual women are said to take on masculine characteristics and wear men's clothing. Further, homosexuals are said to have mental disorders stemming from their sexual orientation. While the first three volumes of the Diagnostic Statistical Manual of Mental Disorders (DSM) classify homosexuality as a personality disorder (Coyle & Kitzinger 2000), researchers have proven otherwise. In 1973, furthermore, the American Psychiatric Association stated that homosexuality was not a mental disorder. It is no longer listed in the DSM-IV as such.

Another empty stereotype is that all incarcerated persons either are or will become homosexual by the time they are released from prison. While homosexual acts do occur in prison, it is wrong to classify all perpetrators as homosexual. Long (1993) discusses three categories of homosexual behavior in the prison population (Haines 1955):

1. The overt ("frank") homosexual who admits his sexual orientation and has feminine mannerisms, speech, and clothing;
2. The psychological homosexual (the feeble-minded, mentally ill, or insane) who are considered aggressive and dangerous; and
3. The situational homosexual who may engage in homosexual behavior when physically threatened or to release sexual frustration or stress. Upon release, situational homosexuals usually experience the most difficulty readjusting to the community; having participated in a behavior condemned by society, they suffer psychological trauma.

In many facilities, gay inmates are placed together. Often, a heterosexual person will request placement in the gay unit, thinking it safer than the general prison population.

Correctional officers in prison, like the general public, call incarcerated homosexuals names such as "fag," "queer," "queen," "punk," and "sissy." They seldom report sexual activity because they feel uncomfortable discussing or writing reports on the incident, they feel that the inmates deserve whatever they get, and they may realize some personal fantasy by watching the sexual act.

Another stereotype is that all gays and lesbians transmit HIV. Unprotected anal (homo or hetero) intercourse leaves a person at high risk of infection, but research has indicated that the spread of the virus is actually decreasing in the gay and lesbian population. It is noteworthy that lesbians seem the lowest at risk. Of major concern, no condoms are used in prison. Safe sex, therefore, is not an option. When the inmate is released, the general population is at risk of HIV transmission.

Gays and Lesbians and Police Encounters

Interactions between police officers and the homosexual population have often involving hostile confrontations. The National Gay and Lesbian Task Force (NGLTF) reported that in some instances, officers are responsible for negative acts and criminal behavior committed against homosexuals. Situations cited range from the use of profanities, refusing to respond when called, and physical beatings. As more officers have been coming out, however, this appears to be changing—police departments, in their increasing diversity, are becoming truly representative of society.

Gay and lesbian police officers are being assigned primarily to gay and lesbian communities. Like the African American police officer culturally matched to the African American community, homosexual officers are considered sell outs; they become, therefore, isolated. Unable to gain a working knowledge of other population segments, their career experiences could be limited. On the other hand, they can assist other police officers in understanding the homosexual culture, and can convince officers to treat homosexuals as they would heterosexuals, with dignity and respect.

Many police officers and criminal justice students do not want to face the issues surrounding gays and lesbians. Newton & Risch (1981) examine why educators need to learn about and discuss homosexuality. Most importantly, increased awareness can save lives. In situations of domestic violence involving same-sex couples, for example, officers often fail to act quickly; as a result, the dispute can result in death. If officers become more aware of their feelings about homosexuals, they might be more inclined to perform their duties in an appropriate manner. Further, as some police officers struggle with their own sexual orientation, studying homosexuality might increase their self-understanding—and, in turn, their understanding of those who are different.

Stonewall Riots

In June 1969, police in New York's Greenwich Village raided gay bars, destroying property and beating and arresting gays. Gays retaliated by throwing rocks, yelling profanities, and setting fires. The Stonewall Inn was burned down, marking the start of the Gay Liberation Movement (Miller 1995).

Although police had raided other gay bars, the brutality and humiliation of the Stonewall incident moved gays to demand human rights. Miller (1995) speculates that the Gay Liberation Movement was motivated by younger gays and lesbians who, having been involved in black student movements and anti-Vietnam demonstrations, were ready to demand their own rights. The Gay Liberation Movement increased public awareness on the plight of gays and lesbians.

Gay Liberation Movement

It is important to explore the liberation of gays and lesbians to understand current issues. Many still believe that granting gays and lesbians equal rights will lead to America's moral and social decline. The Gay Liberation Movement was considered revolutionary in that it advocated abolishing the traditional thinking that only heterosexual behavior was acceptable (Adam 1995, 84). A gay manifesto specifically outlined the aims of the movement, emphasizing resistance to police harassment.

Karl Ulrich, the grandfather of the Gay Liberation Movement, contributed the first scientific literature on homosexuality in Germany in the 1860s. He borrowed the term "Uranian" from Plato to describe same-sex love (Miller 1995). The Society for Human Rights, developed in December 1924 as a result of the work of German American Henry Gerber, was the first organized gay movement in America (Miller 1995).

The Stonewall riots set the machinery in motion; gays organized throughout America. Altman (1980) suggests that a different kind of gay man emerged from the riots—one more self-assertive, capitalistic, and confident (Adam 1995). Police and street violence became more intense after both Stonewall and the assassination of Harvey Milk, a gay San Francisco city councilman, by former police officer Dan White (who was convicted of manslaughter and released after serving five years). During the trial, officers demonstrated in front of the courthouse wearing "Free Dan White" tee shirts (Adam 1995, 114). Instead of covert beatings in alleys, anti-gay groups organized demonstrations and used legislation in their attempts to quell the Gay Liberation Movement.

In an effort to gain rights, gays and lesbians became more politically active; increasing numbers became elected officials, and those in positions of power began coming out. The ACLU became more active, taking gay and lesbian cases to court.

The U.S. Supreme Court has heard two landmark cases regarding homosexual rights. The first, *Bowers v. Hardwick* (1986), involved the 1982 arrest of Michael Hardwick, a gay man. Hardwick was arrested in his bedroom, and charged with violating Georgia's sodomy laws. The Supreme Court ruled homosexual conduct a crime. Most recently, *Romer et al. v. Evans et al.* (1996) struck down *Bowers*. The U.S. Supreme Court, in a six to three decision, affirmed gay and lesbian rights, indicating that discrimination against any group is unconstitutional. This landmark ruling is considered as significant for homosexuals as *Brown v. Board of Education* was for African Americans.

Military

The U.S. military blatantly discriminates against homosexuals (Cruikshank 1992, 11). Military policy states that "homosexuality is incompatible with military service" (Caron 1998), implying that gays and lesbians are unable to reach military standards because of their sexual orientation. It is standard practice to seek out gays and lesbians for purposes of discharge, and to ask enlisting persons to state their sexual orientation (Seidman 1996). While homosexuals with distinguished military records challenge these policies, discrimination continues in law enforcement organizations throughout the country.

In 1992, President Clinton gave the impression that his administration considered ending such discrimination a top priority. He was not, however, able to convince Congress to change the discriminatory codes.

Summary

Of all minorities, homosexuals elicit the least respect and tolerance from police officers and students of criminal justice. This could be due in part to the fact that there is limited positive interaction with this group; fear of the unknown seems to prevail over logic and rational thinking.

Hopefully, this chapter has shed light on an invisible yet prevalent population. It is necessary for students to understand homosexuals' past in order to think critically and dispel stereotypes. Homosexuals are no longer individuals to be whispered about; many hold positions of power. One can come into contact with homosexuals in the work place or at home—they can be mothers, fathers, brothers, sisters, doctors, lawyers, congressional representatives, or police officers.

Key Concepts

Bower v. Hardwick	Homosexuality
Coming Out	Lesbian
Gay	Nature v. Nurture
Gay Liberation Movement	Stonewall Riots

Questions for Discussion

1. Discuss some of the major factors that caused the Stonewall riots. Could the riots have been averted? If so, how? If not, why not?
2. How was the Gay Liberation Movement similar to other civil rights movements?
3. Explain the concept of "coming out." What are some implications?
4. Why do police officers seem to experience the most difficulty working with this segment of the population?
5. What are some implications of the *Goodridge v. Department of Public Health* decision?

Suggested Reading

Berriel, K. 1992. *Dealing with the Criminal Justice System*. Washington, DC: National Gay and Lesbian Task Force.

Gross, L. 1996. Identity politics, coming out, and coming together. In M. Rodgers (Ed.), *Multiculturalism Experiences and Multiculturalism Theory*. New York, NY: McGraw Hill Publishers.

<http://www.actwin.com/eatonohio/gay/GAY.htm>. A website on gay rights information and legislation passed or currently in debate in Congress.

<www.hrc.org>. This is the Human Rights Campaign website where a detailed page of the "Don't Ask, Don't Tell" policy of 1993 can be found and what affects it has on military personnel.

<www.psychpage.com/learning/library/gay/comeout.html>. This website discusses the stages of "coming out" as a gay individual.

CHAPTER 10

POLICING ASIAN AMERICANS

Learning Objectives

1. Explain why Asian Americans are considered an in-between minority.
2. Discuss why Asian Americans are reluctant to report crimes.
3. Identify some strategies that police officers can use when working with Asian Americans.
4. Discuss the impact of the Chinese Exclusion Act.
5. Discuss the short and long term effects of Executive Order 9066 on Japanese Americans.

Historical Perspective

While federal statistics identify over thirty-two Asian American groups, representing 4.2 percent of the U.S. population (Grieco & Cassidy 2001), Americans lump them into a homogenous, un-American group based on physical characteristics. Even the most familiar Asian Americans (e.g., Chinese, Japanese, Filipinos, Asian Indians, Koreans, Pacific Islanders, and Southeast Asians) are called Chinese or Japanese.

Asian Americans, like other minority groups, have had to face discrimination grounded in racism and resentment of their success (Benson 2003). Many Americans are biased because of Asian Americans' high standardized test scores (Segal 2002) and business savvy, especially in the electronics and automotive industries—they fail to realize that it is usually Asians, not Asian Americans, behind these successes (Wu & Song 2000). Discrimination manifests itself in racial slurs, physical attacks, college admissions, and inaccurate stereotypes of unhygienic standards of cleanliness (Kitano & Daniels 2001).

Asians migrated to America for economic and educational opportunities, contract labor, to escape political turmoil, and as refugees (Kitano & Daniels 2001). During the nineteenth century, Asian Americans (particularly those of Chinese extraction) were welcomed as miners and railroad builders. When their services were no longer required, however, whites grew concerned with their continuing influx (Kitano & Daniels 2001), fearing economic competition. Lynchings and killings began.

By the mid 1800s, new and revised anti-Chinese laws emerged, institutionalizing the racism. Asian Americans were stripped of rights—they couldn't attend school, testify in court, or own their own businesses. Further, they suffered extensive job discrimination (Flowers 1988, 14). Like African Americans, Chinese were beaten and murdered with few, if any, consequences brought against the perpetrators.

The Chinese Exclusion Act of 1882 legitimized these discriminatory practices by blocking Chinese entry into America for a ten year period; Chinese were the largest Asian American group and the only minority ever legally banned from entry (Wong 1995). With the act in place, other laborers were brought in to work (e.g., Koreans, Japanese, and Asian Indians) (Min 1995).

Kitano & Daniels (2001) identify the racist fears that led to the Exclusion Act's passage and, twenty years later, its indefinite extension—loss of jobs, physical differences, and the Asian culture. Threatened by Asian workers, whites called them "heathens" or "yellow dogs," criticized their customs, restricted their movements, and exploited and dehumanized Asian American women.

Alongside such blatant racism, institutional discrimination peaked in 1907 and 1924 with the enactment of formal agreements and immigration laws. In 1907, the U.S. and Japan drafted the Gentleman's Agreement to restrict Japanese immigration of workers (skilled or unskilled) into the U.S. In return for the Japanese agreeing to restrict their people by not issuing them passports to the U.S., Roosevelt agreed that he would not allow the passage of laws discriminating against Japanese immigrants. While President Wilson tried to honor this agreement, the U.S. imposed a literacy test in 1917 (immigrants must be able to read English) for immigrants over sixteen years of age; Asians, unable to meet these standards, were denied entry.

The Immigration Act of 1924, often referred to as the first act to establish a quota system based on national origins (allowing only 150,000 entry), was even more restrictive and lasted until 1952. Celler (1953) suggests that this action occurred because of America's distrust of Japanese and Chinese. Still, Asians were denied citizenship. In a landmark court case, Ozawa v. U.S. (1922), the U.S. Supreme Court ruled that Japanese could not attain U.S. citizenship because they were not black or white (Nishi 1995, 102). Finally, the 1943 Magnuson Act qualified Chinese for citizenship for political rather than humanitarian reasons (Wong 1995, 65)—because China had been an American ally in WWII, the U.S. Government felt the need to demonstrate friendship (Kitano & Daniels 2001). In 1946, Congress lifted the quota on Asian immigration by allowing entry to war brides and children of American soldiers. In 1952, then, the McCarran Walter Bill (that became the Immigration and Nationality Act), made it possible for all races (including Asians), meeting specific criteria, to become citizens (Kitano & Daniels 2001).

Changes in immigration laws have impacted society's Asian American composition. The Immigration Act of 1965 led to a new wave of Asian immigration (Chuman 1976). Specifically, the act abolished the national origin and race quota system, and established the allocation of immigrant visas on a first come, first serve basis. The act attempted to eliminate discrimination based on origin by lessening the restrictions on Asian immigration provided that they possessed needed skills (occupational immigration), had relatives in the U.S. (family reunification), or were escaping political and/or religious persecution (asylum) (Wu & Song 2000).

Asian immigration increased again during the 1970s (especially from the Philippines and South Korea) (Min 1995), and the 1980s (from China, India, and Vietnam). These increases were primarily due to the Displaced Persons Act of 1948 that allowed refugees (especially Koreans and Vietnamese) entry (Kitano & Daniels 2001) and allowed those already in America to remain (Wong 1995). The Immigration Act of 1990 amended the Immigration Act of 1965, liberalizing immigration laws (Segal 2002, 153) and resulting in an influx of Asians for employment purposes. The 1990 Immigration Act, then, revised all grounds for exclusion and deportation. The admission of communists as nonimmigrants was repealed, and the Attorney General was given authority to grant temporary protected status to undocumented alien nationals.

Immigration issues have always prompted debate in America. The Statute of Liberty stands with open arms and the words "give me your tired, your poor, your huddled masses yearning to breathe free" at its feet, symbolizing America is a nation of immigrants. At the same time, however, there has been a constant stream of restrictive laws, policies, and events (Mintz 2003), as shown in Table 10.1.

U.S. immigration policies have been criticized for displaying favoritism toward Europeans and discriminating against people of color. Minority groups, however, are growing fast; indeed, these groups will become the majority by the year 2030. It is anticipated, however, that the current "alert" status in the wake

Table 10.1

Immigration Act. January 29, 1795.	Restricted citizenship to free white persons who resided in the U.S. for five years and who renounced their countries of origin.
Alien Enemy Act. July 6, 1798.	Extended the minimum residency requirement for citizenship to fourteen years. A separate Alien Act valid only until 1800 empowered the President to punish traitorous activity on the part of non-naturalized individuals by deportation.
Naturalization Act. April 14, 1802.	Reduced the minimum residency requirement for citizenship to five years.
Act Prohibiting Importation of Slaves. January 1, 1808.	Prohibited the importation of slaves.
Irish Potato Famine. 1840.	Period of massive Irish immigration.
Gold Rush. 1849.	Period of massive Chinese immigration.
July 4, 1864.	A Bureau of Immigration was established to promote immigration during the Civil War.
Naturalization Act. July 12, 1870.	Extended the Naturalization law to include immigrants from Africa and those of African descent.
Immigration Act. March 3, 1875.	For the first time, a federal law excluded certain groups of immigrants: prostitutes, and Chinese contract workers ("Coolies").
Chinese Exclusion Act. May 6, 1882.	Restricted Chinese immigration.
Immigration Act. February 26, 1885.	Forbade the importation of contract laborers (except domestic servants and doctors).

Table 10.1 (*continued*)

Immigration Act. March 3, 1891.	Excluded the mentally ill and those incapable of earning a living from immigration.
Ellis Island. January 1, 1892.	Opened as a federal immigration station.
Anarchist Exclusion Act. September 14, 1901.	Excluded immigrants on the basis of their political opinions.
Immigration Act. March, 1903.	Barred anarchists and desirables from immigration.
Gentleman's Agreement. March 14, 1907.	The Japanese agreed not to issue sailing permits for Japanese workers.
Immigration Act. February 5, 1917.	Immigrants had to be able to speak and read English to be admitted.
Immigration Act. May 22, 1918.	Proponents to overthrow the U.S. government were barred from immigration.
Quota Law. May 19, 1921.	Limited the annual number of immigrants: 200,000 from Northwest Europe, 155,000 from East and South Europe, and 1,000 from Asia and Africa.
Quota Law #2. May 26, 1924.	Limited visas to those who could become a welfare burden.
Quota Law #3. March 4, 1929.	Identified deportable offenses: carrying weapons, bombs, and violating prohibition.
The Alien Registration or Smith Act. June 28, 1940.	Foreigners had to be fingerprinted. The President could deport foreigners suspected of espionage.
Executive Order 9066. February 19, 1942.	Authorized the military to evacuate over 112,000 Japanese Americans from the Pacific Coast and place them in ten internment camps.

Table 10.1 (*continued*)

The Magnuson Act. December 17, 1943.	Repealed the Chinese Exclusion Act of 1882.
War Brides Act. December 28, 1945.	Waived visa requirements and some provisions of the immigration law for armed forces members who married nationals.
The Displaced Persons Act. June 25, 1948.	Permitted the immigration of over four hundred thousand Europeans until 1952. Permitted exceptions for refugees in dire need.
The Internal Security Act (a.k.a. McCarron Act). September 22, 1950.	Barred admission to any foreigner who was a communist or who might engage in activities endangering the welfare of the U.S.
The Refugee Relief Act. August 7, 1953.	Extended immigration into America, over and above the previously established quota system, and extended refugee status to non-Europeans.
Cuban Refugee Act. November 2, 1966.	Permitted over four hundred thousand Cubans and Puerto Ricans to enter the U.S.
Immigration Act. March 17, 1980.	Enacted a response to the boat people fleeing Vietnam; granted asylum to politically oppressed refugees.
Immigration Act. November 6, 1986.	Granted amnesty to three million undocumented residents.
The Redress Act or Civil Liberties Act. August 10, 1988.	Provided twenty thousand dollars compensation to survivors of the WWII Internment of Japanese and Japanese Americans.
Immigration Act. November 29, 1990.	Increased the number of immigrants allowed into the U.S.

Table 10.1 (*continued*)

The Illegal Immigration Reform & Immigrant Responsibility Act. September 30, 1996.	Strengthened the border enforcement and made it more difficult to gain asylum.
Nicaraguan Adjustment & Central American Relief Act. November 19, 1997.	Provided relief from the deportation of certain Nicaraguans, Cubans, Salvadorans, and Guatemalans.
The American Competitiveness & Work Force Improvement Act. March 20, 1998.	Increased the number of skilled temporary foreign workers that employers were allowed to bring into the U.S.
Memorial Honoring Japanese Americans. June 29, 2001.	A memorial honoring Japanese American veterans and detainees was opened in DC.

of 9/11 will result in tighter immigration laws. It is crucial that, even in such a state of preparedness, the U.S not get involved in more internment camps.

Executive Order 9066

On February 19, 1942, President Roosevelt issued Executive Order 9066, stipulating the rounding up of persons of Japanese ancestry living on the West Coast (excluding Hawaii, not yet a U.S. state, where the U.S. Government simply declared martial law in order to control the Japanese population) to be placed in a "military area." These relocation centers, or concentration camps, resembled German concentration camps with their armed guards, razor wire fences, and orders to "shoot to kill" anyone trying to escape. Executive Order 9066 directly violated the U.S. Constitution—most of those incarcerated were American citizens (who happened to be of Japanese heritage) not formally charged with any crime, not granted access to an attorney, not allowed a trial by an impartial jury, and exposed to cruel and unusual punishment (Wong 1996). These relocation centers have been described as second only to slavery in their harshness (Kitano & Daniels 2001).

In 1976, President Gerald Ford repealed Executive Order 9066 and formed the Commission on Wartime Relocation and Internment of Civilians (CWRIC) to assess the circumstances that had led to placing Japanese Americans in camps. The commission concluded that Congress should formally apologize to Japanese Americans, and the U.S. Government would compensate each surviving victim with twenty thousand dollars. In 1988, the majority of the commission's suggestions became law (Kitano & Daniels 2001).

Family Values

While Asian Americans are not homogenous, they share common values (Min 1995). In the traditional Asian family hierarchy, for example, the father and oldest son are the primary authority figures, and females are subordinate. In Asian American families, too, rules and responsibilities are clearly delineated—women are expected to do household chores, while men work and act as the authority figure. Divorce rates among Asian couples are similar to white Americans, but Asian Americans dislike outsiders intervening in family situations.

Respect and caring for elders is fundamental. The sandwich generation (when primary care providers care for their own children as well as for their parents) is a familiar concept to Asian American families, as they have been caring for elderly family members for generations. Traditionally, the greater the number of family members indicated more prosperity (Min 1995). Additionally, Confucius guided Asian thinking (especially Chinese) in extending the family to include kinship groups and clan members (Wong 1995, 68).

Asian Americans place great value on education. Children are expected to perform well at school, preferably in science and math. Poor performance is a family embarrassment.

The traditional family, however, is eroding—Shibutani & Kwan (1956) suggest that acculturation and intermarriage (Segal 2002) will cause Asian Americans to abandon their traditions and become biologically and psychologically assimilated ("Americanized"). Wong (1995) suggests that many Asian Americans, as they acculturate, will think more like Americans than like Asians.

To be sure, inter-generational conflict is increasing between Americanized Asian children and their traditional parents (Chen 1995). Children, trying to fit into their predominantly white peer groups while simultaneously adhering to traditional Asian customs, experience confusion and frustration. As children have become more Americanized, gender roles have changed. More Asian American women are entering the work force, which means more Asian American children in day care and more Asian American elderly in nursing homes. Further, fewer speak their traditional language in the home.

Asian American families favor the Democratic Party (Kitano & Daniels 2001), yet are considered conservative. Some Asian Americans have held congressional seats—most famous are Daniel Inouye of Hawaii, and Spark Matsunaga, who sponsored numerous human service bills. Today, Asian Americans are winning important seats in local politics.

Stereotypes

Asian Americans have been stereotyped the "model minority" (Lien 2001) because so many have been academically successful. Society, however, fails to realize that for many who live in poverty and cannot speak English, this stereotype is a burden. Some, for example, are denied federal assistance because agency representatives consider them least in need (Min 1995).

While Asian Americans are stereotyped as alike socially, politically, and economically, they can actually be divided into "haves" and "have-nots." The haves sit at the top of the economic hierarchy (e.g., Japanese, Chinese), and the larger group, the "have-nots," at the bottom (e.g., Vietnamese, Filipinos). Differences are based on occupations (except for the Vietnamese and Filipinos, Asian Americans have attained high rank in the corporate world) and education levels (Vietnamese and Filipinos do not exceed the average education level as do other Asian groups) (Marger 1994, 342).

Asian Americans are often called "Japs," "Chinks," or "Slant Eyes." Most Americans see them as Chinese or Japanese, and believe that they eat domestic animals like cats or dogs. The media has provided yet another stereotype—street gangs and Asian mafia.

Asian Indians (often called "Hindoos"), undergo a slightly different experience. Because they are often mistaken for Hispanics or African Americans, they tend to be stereotyped as cheap motel or convenient store operators.

Asian crime rates may be hidden because of Asians' "close communities" (Flowers 1988, 190), or discreetness. Chinese organized crime, however, exists; Flowers (1988) claims that the Chinese Tongs (a.k.a. Triads), a secret society with criminal enterprises, entered the U.S. early and became entrenched in Chinatowns across the nation (Kitano & Daniels 2001). While the Tongs initially protected the Chinese community from racist attacks (Wong 2005), their criminal activities overshadow their paternalistic behavior. Law enforcement has had difficulty filing charges against members primarily because they play such major roles in the Chinese community (Wong 2005). Like the Italian Mafia, the Triads take care of their own without need of police or court intervention. Kitano & Daniels (1988) discuss the various Asian mafias such as the Japanese Yakuza, the Chinese Triads, and Korean and Vietnamese gangs. The typical Asian American mafia member is thought to be a businessman in a limo surrounded by blonde women and Asian men. Some non-Asian Americans believe that the Asian mafia will soon own America.

Asian Americans and Law Enforcement

According to the Uniform Crime Report, Asian crime rates are low compared with other groups. Just as overall crime rates have increased, however, so have they risen in this population—an increase that can be attributed to drugs, unemployment, and an organized crime connection between Asia and America. The increase is seen not only in Asian organized crime, but also in juvenile crime. Chinese juvenile gangs are said to be employers of the Chinese Tong. Because of language barriers, unemployment, drugs, cultural adjustment difficulties, and feelings of alienation, youths became involved in delinquent activities such as purse snatching, extortion, and robbery (Flowers 1988, 139).

The conflict between Asian and African Americans has intensified, as the latter group feels intimidated by Asian businesses. During the 1992 Los Angeles riots, many Chinese and Japanese Americans wanted it known that they were separate from Koreans because of the tension existing between Koreans and African Americans (Chang & Oh 1995, 135). This conflict provoked increased media attention and awareness of the Korean population, subsequently intensifying law enforcement within Asian American communities—a change that has angered many Asian Americans because they prefer, and feel able to, handle their problems without outside involvement. Wong (1996) explains how this reluctance to call on police may be cultural; in many Asian countries, police are corrupt and nothing gets done without some form of payment (graft). The reluctance may also stem from the difficulties Asian Americans have experienced in interacting with police officers both because of the language barrier and because many officers (veterans of wars involving Asians) treat them like military prisoners. Finally, Asian Americans may not know their rights as U.S. residents.

Asian Americans are also targets for hate crimes, for the following reasons:

1. The growth of the Asian American population;
2. Economic factors such as the trade deficit;
3. Increased numbers of corporations (e.g., automobile manufactures) closing means greater competition for jobs;

4. Conflict with African Americans;
5. The escalating conflicts in China and North Korea; and
6. The success image. Asian Americans establish more businesses in African American communities.

Shusta et al. (1995) identify the following factors that police officers should be aware of when dealing with Asian Americans:

1. Asian Americans are a heterogeneous group. Officers should not imply otherwise.
2. Officers should acknowledge and make use of the extended family network. Children, for example, often act as interpreters for adults. At the same time, officers will have to be cognizant of the content of what they ask the child to interpret (e.g., sexual issues embarrass the child). To avoid being considered rude, officers should address the adult even though the child may be translating.
3. When an Asian American says "no" to someone in authority it is considered impolite and results in a "loss of face." When they answer "yes," the implication can be "yes but I may or may not agree," or "I may or may not do what I understand," or "I may not agree," or "I will do what you suggested." It is important, therefore, that officers are clear about the meaning of "yes."
4. Eye contact with someone in authority is considered disrespectful. Police officers, therefore, should not consider the lack of eye contact a sign of guilt.
5. While Asian Americans may show no facial expressions in emotional situations, this does not mean that they are not experiencing stress.
6. Officers should not be embarrassed to ask an Asian American his identity of preference. Some Asians, for example, do not like being called Orientals.

Summary

This chapter aimed to: 1) provide a general awareness of the Asian American experience in the hopes that criminal justice students and police officers will further explore the similarities and differences existing within the group, 2) consider how Asian American experiences in society may impact relations with law enforcement, and 3) provide the information needed to assist students in considering strategies to enhance Asian American/police relations.

Key Concepts

Anti-Chinese

Chinese Exclusion Act

Chinese Tongs

Executive Order 9066

Magnuson Act 1943

Model Minority Immigration Act 1965

Ozawa v. U.S. Gentlemen's Agreement

Relocation Camps

Questions for Discussion

1. Discuss why some feel that U.S. immigration policies have been discriminatory.
2. Discuss hate crimes involving Asian Americans. How were the situations resolved?
3. Explain why Asian Indians are considered separate from other Asian American groups. Identify the stereotypical thinking.
4. Explain how the immigration acts were significant to Asian Americans.
5. Discuss why Asian Americans may feel apprehensive or hostile toward law enforcement officers.

Suggested Reading

Harman, A. 1993. Battling organized asian crime gangs. *Law and Order*, 4(12), 51–54.

Song, J. 1992. Attitudes of chinese immigrants and vietnamese refugees toward law enforcement in the u.s. *Justice Quarterly*, 9(4), 703–719.

<www.aalea.org>. Asian American Law Enforcement Association.

<www.census.gov/population/www/socdemo/race/api.html>. This is the current population survey of Asians and Pacific Islanders.

<www.naaalec.org/History.htm>. National Association of Asian Americans Law Enforcement Commanders.

<www.napalc.org>. National Asian Pacific American Legal Consortium.

Chapter 11

Policing Adolescent Street Gangs

Learning Objectives

1. Discuss the factors that allow a gang to take over a community.
2. Explain why street gangs are so prevalent in society.
3. Discuss how gangs differ.
4. Explain what law enforcement can do to control gangs.
5. Discuss what programs, if any, might deter a youth from joining a gang.

Historical Perspective

Gangs have existed in America since colonial days. Early gangs consisted of individuals who joined with a common goal. The term "gang," however, is ambiguous; even researchers have been unable to agree on a definition (Knox 2000). Some might call the framers of the U.S. Constitution a gang because their behavior involved secrecy, a common goal, and confrontations.

Other groups and individuals could similarly fall into this category, yet Americans have accepted their behavior as "normal" or even glorified their malicious acts. College fraternities recruit, haze, use hand signals, and wear identifying colors (Jackson 1989). Jesse James' gang received notoriety for its robberies and murders. Further, the media sensationalized gang activity with the operations of Al Capone and Charles Manson. The leading gangs of the 1980s and 1990s (the Bloods, the Crips, and the Latin Kings), however, differed in their use of more serious weaponry and their involvement in criminal activities.

For our purposes, we will use the definition accepted by law enforcement officers—a gang is a cohesive group (three or more individuals) coming together on a regular basis for the purpose of planning and implementing criminal activity (Goldstein & Huff 1993).

American gangs (especially Hispanic gangs) can be traced back to 1927 (Thrasher 1927). It is important to recognize that gangs differ. African American gangs such as the Bloods and the Crips, for example, are considered transitional because of their short life span (approximately thirty years), Hispanic gangs are considered traditional because they can be traced back three or four generations, and Asian gangs are more difficult to classify and describe both because the Asian culture withholds information (especially regarding criminal activity) from outsiders, and early exclusion immigration policies resulted in there being fewer Asian American adolescents (Goldstein & Huff 1993).

While many gangs exist, it has been difficult to acquire accurate statistics on their numbers, activities, and locations. Over one hundred thousand Crips and Bloods, for example, are said to be in the Los Angeles area alone (Maxson et al. 1998). Even the Gang Reporting Evaluation and Tracking (GREAT) information system, developed in the 1980s for the purpose of collecting gang data, has been unable to provide accurate information. Three reasons are offered. First, gangs have become mobile. Second, higher-level gang members are not easily identified. Third, some adolescents may have been identified as members when, in fact, they were not.

Why Do Children Join Gangs?

Children join gangs for many reasons. The following are some of the reasons provided by gang members:

1. "I'm bored." Especially in small towns, children join gangs for the excitement.
2. "My mother's not home so I hang out." In many single parent households, the mother has to work and has little time to spend with her family. Children can feel isolated and in need of attention or someone with whom they can discuss concerns.
3. "To help my mother at home." This can mean monetary assistance, protection from an abusive husband or boyfriend, or handling household responsibilities.
4. "To be with my friends." Peer pressure is a strong motivator.
5. "So that I won't have to take stuff from nobody." Membership provides a sense of power; adolescents can instill fear into others by their mere

presence. Further, it offers a sense of security, knowing that others will "watch your back."

6. "To look good." Gang membership builds self-esteem; this is powerful to those children whose teachers have deemed them "unreachable" (out of control, unable to learn, and bound for failure). These children feel good wearing gang colors, and accomplishing tasks for the gang (unfortunately, usually criminal in nature).

7. "They my family." Gang membership provides family for children surviving on their own and even supporting others.

Gang Communication Methods

Gang members communicate through graffiti, flashing (hand signs), gear (clothing), and body markings.

Graffiti (hit-up or tag)

Graffiti is one of the most crucial methods of communicating among gang members. Indeed, graffiti was the primary means of communication before the rise of the Internet. Police officers should look for it as it identifies not only the gang, but any rivals vying for control, gang deaths, and those members targeted for revenge. It is also used to welcome visiting members.

Graffiti varies depending on the gang's cultural background. Hispanic graffiti, for example, is bright and colorful and uses large lettering, while African American graffiti is simple and direct and uses only the gang's color (or black spray paint).

Flashing (a.k.a. tossin'-it-up or rollin)

Hand signals are used for identification, sending messages across a room, or to challenge an opponent. These signals are almost identical to the American Sign Language (Capozzoli & McVey 2000), different only in style or flow of presentation. Often, tossin'-up one's hood is best done to rap music; an observer might think that the person was dancing.

Gear (Clothing)

Members wear gang colors only when they are seeking a rival or are involved in an activity crucial to their credibility—otherwise, they wear neutral colors (e.g., beige or khaki pants with a white or black shirt) to avoid identification by the police. The Latin Kings, for example, wear black when not geared up. Different sets identify themselves by wearing specific jackets, caps, and sneakers (with shoelaces of a certain color and tied in a distinctive manner). Members avoid rival colors—Bloods, for example, never wear blue because it is a Crip color, or British Knights sneakers, the Crips' footwear.

Body Markings

Some gangs use tattoos as a means of identification. Hispanic members, for example, might cover their arms, shoulders, and back. Tattoos range from large displays to a small dot in the palm of the hand. African American gangs use tattoos to a lesser degree; theirs are usually more personalized (e.g., gang name).

Stereotypes

The media has glorified gang activity. While gangs have always existed in America, they seem to have grown in number and influence every time a television program or movie is aired. Gang stereotypes include:

1. Gangs are all alike. In reality, gangs struggle to maintain differences among sets.
2. Gangs have only male members. Not only do female gangs exist, but are considered, by some, more violent than their male counterparts (Capozzoli & McVey 2000).
3. All gang members are involved with drugs.
4. Gangs are disorganized groups of uneducated children. In truth, gangs are highly organized—many are backed by unaffiliated adults (even, at times, by some law enforcement personnel).
5. Gang members do not want to work, and hang out on street corners. Some members are either in school, or are seeking employment. If jobs are available, many choose to work.
6. Once a gang member, always a gang member. This is a common misunderstanding. The saying merely means that while a member can physically leave a gang, some of the conditioning that accompanied recruitment remains with the person.

Law Enforcement Preventive Measures

Often, local city councils and commissioners fail to act until gang activity is beyond prevention—at which point, control measures have little or no effect. This political denial hinders law enforcement officers in controlling gangs.

Gaining Control of the Community

How does a gang take control of a new territory? The following phases—assessment, recruitment, and gangbanging I and II—are unique to Bloods and Crips.

Assessment Phase

During this phase, members are sent into prospective cities to "scope the area" and determine the feasibility of becoming established. Considerations include the strength of law enforcement, the composition of the community, and the availability of resources.

The strength of law enforcement varies, depending on firepower (type of guns used), the number of police officers, policy on the necessity of vests, the type of patrol (cars, bikes, or foot), patrol patterns, officer ages, and the strength of the police-community relationship. Gang members also observe officers' tactics and demeanors to determine whether they operate legally or illegally (Jackson 2003).

Gang members either move quickly into a community, or they establish a relationship with a resident who supplies information on existing leaders and criminal activities. Members might observe the community and profile its residents. Mr. X, for example, sits on his porch every night from ten o'clock until midnight. If Mr. X has a positive relationship with the police, action will be taken to change his habit. If Mr. X has a poor relationship, however, the gang will consider him a potential "look out." Businesses, churches, and schools are likewise observed to determine the nature of their interactions with residents and police. Children experiencing family or school problems are targeted.

Gangs assess community resources to determine what can be used to meet their objectives and what can be used against them. Factors include:

1. Military bases.
2. Rival gangs. The gang determines if they are willing to initiate an altercation to remove any opponents (is the territory worthwhile monetarily?), or if they can coexist.

3. Political atmosphere. Is there a "get tough on gangs" police chief and/or mayor? Are they proactive or reactive?
4. Demand for drugs. Are there many elementary and middle schools? Are there colleges and universities?

Recruitment Phase

When police officers consider gang recruitment, they often think of adolescents. Recruitment, however, begins with adults, and is a deliberate process that can take up to a year. The first new member is usually a woman able to move freely through the community, thereby helping the recruiter become established. This woman is typically an unemployed single parent of three or four children. Recently, however, gangs have moved in on women employed in low-paying jobs in gas stations or fast food restaurants.

Recruitment of adolescents follows—ideally young men who "strut their stuff," do not fear authority figures, and can further the gang's cause. Targets are given simple assignments, and undergo loyalty tests. Backed by the gang recruiter, they are reinforced with rewards, including money or expensive sporting apparel. When they perform poorly, the recruiter instructs them on alternative methods; they then repeat the tasks until successful.

This group of ten to twenty adolescents becomes the core group, and begins recruiting younger children (eight to ten year-olds) using these same methods. This process ensures the perpetuation of the particular set (individual gang unit).

Bangin' Phase I (activity phase)

This phase has two major components: 1) the honeymoon phase in which activity is staged on a non-lethal level, involving writing graffiti messages and making drug deliveries, and 2) setting the stage for open recruitment. Members are taught to hate rivals and protect their "hoods" by any means necessary. Graffiti welcomes members of affiliate sets, calls for war, or simply marks turf. Members hang out where other adolescents will see them (e.g., malls, movies, schools). They get noticed by police officers, and often challenge them by staring them down—an encounter that sets the tone for the member's future interaction with law enforcement.

Open recruitment begins when gang markings become visible in schools. Other adolescents may know the identity of the early recruits, but teachers only see some children acting out and cannot understand the reason. Schools, therefore, should hire a resource officer who can proactively prevent gang activity.

Bangin' Phase II

This phase, consisting of violent physical acts such as drive-by shootings or severe beatings (beating a person down), is the most crucial. It is also the most visible; by the time police officers see and try to control the situation, however, it is already out of hand.

There is a constant power struggle between the gang, its rivals, and the police. By this point, the community has lost control—still, even without strong parental involvement, the community can influence gang members. In areas where parents and relatives rose through the gang ranks (original gangsters (OGs)), however, there is a more deeply entrenched hold on the community.

Law Enforcement Interactions with Gang Members

Police officers should study gang activity before formulating for a plan to combat the problem. When trying to eliminate or control gang activity, for example, it is a good strategy to develop a relationship with an associate (a member not directly involved in violent activity) or a peripheral member (a "wanta be"/"wanna bee" who has not undergone initiation or taken the oath of loyalty). This initial contact is usually most beneficial if the officer assumes an attitude of inquiry rather than acting as if he/she has all the answers. Officers who work with these youths are more successful than those who use scare tactics, as such tactics are less frightening than those used by gangs. At times, peripherals can even be prevented from becoming members.

Lieutenant Wright, when working with the Los Angeles police department, stated that gangsters used to have some respect for police officers, but now have only "malice and contempt" (Sturdivant 1994). This thinking stems from an incident in which two officers in Compton, California (the gang capital) were brutally gunned down. Indeed, Compton police boards are covered with articles detailing officer assassinations (Senna & Seigel 1994).

The Compton gang unit, when under the leadership of Chief Taylor and Lieutenant Wright, offered the following advice regarding gang interactions:

1. Police officers should become more involved in the community, including schools, churches, and local businesses. They should work cooperatively to educate not only gang members, but parents and children who are at risk of joining.

2. Police officers should increase and improve verbal communication with gang members.
3. Computer technology (and a database) is essential, as it enables police officers to track members.
4. Police officers should communicate more with each other and with officers in other jurisdictions.
5. Police officers should use community oriented policing as a means of reducing gang violence.

Gang members will leave gangs if they can find something providing them with equal motivation. Many members age out of gang activity, but still hold an allegiance to the colors. Some millionaire rap and hip-hop recording artists like Snoop Doggy Dog and Ice-T., for example, still engage in gang subculture behaviors—for example, they might wear only gang colors at performances.

Law enforcement faces a real dilemma in dealing with gangs because they themselves function like a gang (Jackson 2003). A number of special law enforcement gang units (e.g., California, Florida) have been dismantled because officers were using violent gang-like tactics and mishandling evidence in their efforts to suppress street gangs. Still, it is important to understand that officers are considered a legal gang (Jackson 2003); they must be careful not to cross the line.

Summary

Gangs have existed in America since colonial days. While methods of operation may have changed, their goals remain the same. The drug economy and media hype have played vital roles in increasing gang activity. Myths exist regarding gang members: they are illiterate, uncontrollable, disorganized, and easily identified. Working cooperatively with community residents (schools, businesses, churches, law enforcement organizations, and parents), these youths can be redirected—many "OGs," for example, now work in "respectable" business establishments.

Key Concepts

Assessment Phase	Gang Bangin'
Flashing	Gear
Gaining Control	Graffiti
Gang	OGs

Questions for Discussion

1. Discuss strategies that communities can use to reduce gang activity.

2. Explain some intervention strategies that communities have used to deter gang activity. Consider your own community and a neighboring community.

3. Discuss the characteristics of gangs in general, then select two specific gangs to compare and contrast.

4. What are some strategies that officers can use to control or reduce gang violence?

5. Discuss programs that might be helpful to youth who are at risk of joining a gang. Explain how some programs can be instrumental in getting youths to quit the gang.

Suggested Reading

Jackson, M.S. 2003. Law enforcement's response to illegal street gang activity. In A.R. Roberts (Ed.), *Critical Issues in Crime and Justice*. Thousand Oaks, CA: Sage Publications.

Reese, R. 2004. *American Paradox: Young Black Men*. Durham, NC: Carolina Academic Press.

<www.jibc.bc.ca/Libraryfiles/archive/PDFDownloads/Bibliographies/GANGS. pdf>. A good introduction and bibliography on youth gangs in America.

<http://ojjdp.ncjrs.org/pubs/gun_violence/profile22.html>. Prevention strategies used to avoid adolescents joining street gangs.

<www.safeyouth.org/topics/gangs.htm>. Posted by the National Youth Violence Resource Prevention Center. Covers all aspects of adolescent gangs in America.

CHAPTER 12

FUTURE TRENDS IN POLICING AND IMPLICATIONS

Learning Objectives

1. Discuss five pros and cons of the Crime Bill.
2. Discuss five pros and cons of affirmative action.
3. Consider what plans other than affirmative action would guarantee equal opportunity for citizens in employment, education, and housing.
4. Discuss at least five methods for improving police-minority relations.
5. Discuss the legal, social, and political implications of affirmative action.

Crime Bill

On September 13, 1994, President Clinton signed the Violent Crime Control and Law Enforcement Act (Crime Bill). The Crime Bill includes the following major provisions:

- One hundred thousand more law enforcement officers;
- More stringent penalties for repeat offenders (Three Strikes);
- More stringent penalties for hate crime offenders;
- Increased death penalty sanctions for more crime categories;
- Crime increased gang penalties; and
- Increased penalties for crimes against women.

The Crime Bill grew out of the 1980s "get tough on crime" philosophy (increasing apprehension and arrest rates to reduce crime). Opposite to the due process model, this crime control model presumes the defendant guilty until proven innocent. The current conservative Supreme Court under Chief Justice William Rehnquist ascribes to this get-tough model; it is likely, therefore, that laws will be enacted for years to come based on this policy. Most of the 1980s get-tough anti-crime legislation was enacted under the auspices of the anti-drug laws. Interestingly, however, as arrest rates climbed, there was little decrease in criminal activity. It remains to be seen whether this trend will continue as the new Crime Bill takes effect.

More Law Enforcement Officers

The Crime Bill will allow for the recruiting, hiring, rehiring (where law enforcement officers have been laid off due to budgetary restraints), and training of officers with an emphasis on community policing. This strategy, in which police officers work with the community to resolve crime problems, is meant to serve as a crime prevention tool.

Three Strikes

When a person convicted of two serious felonies is convicted of a third, life imprisonment is automatically sought under the Three Strikes rule. Like other law enforcement policies, this rule is not effective on Indian reservations. Further, if a person sentenced under the Three Strikes rule reaches age seventy after serving at least thirty years, he can be released (Reid 1998).

Some states (e.g., California) adopted the Three Strikes policy prior to federal enactment; still more have begun implementing it now. While the plan initially seemed a good idea to many police officers, citizens, and politicians, its cost is proving both unmanageable for many states and imprudent to many judges (who must enforce the sanction even when an offender is undeserving). Prisons will have to be built to accommodate offenders. To further complicate matters, the Supreme Court has ruled laws allowing life sentences for a third felony constitutional (*Ewing v. California, Lockyer v. Andrade*).

Hate Crimes

Hate crimes, on the increase for years, are an important part of the Crime Bill. Hate crimes are defined as those perpetrated onto others because of race, nationality, origin, religion, gender, sexual orientation, age, or creed (Siasoco 1999). As a result of the Crime Bill, federal sanctions have increased, and penalties are more stringent.

Death Penalty

The death penalty has been historically limited to federal crimes involving drug-related homicides and hijackings. Now the list of offenses has increased to include large amounts of drug trafficking, drive-by shootings, carjackings resulting in death, and genocide. Federal law prohibits the use of capital punishment in cases involving the mentally retarded, pregnant women, anyone under eighteen years old, and wherever racial discrimination is involved.

Increased Gang Penalties

The Crime Bill provides for harsher punishment against gangs so as to send a strong message to youths that gangs, guns, and drugs will not be tolerated. The bill bans the use of handguns by juveniles, promises harsh punishment for those gang members involved in criminal activities, and calls for the establishment of youth drug courts in addition to the controversial boot camps (limited evaluation research is available regarding their advantages or disadvantages).

The Crime Bill mirrors popular opinion about delinquents—today, a conservative attitude compared with the former liberal thinking that juveniles who committed criminal offenses needed treatment and rehabilitation rather than punishment. While the juvenile crime rate has declined, however, there has been an increase in the serious violent crimes, and the offenders have become younger. In response, the Crime Bill included provisions for youths thirteen years and over to be tried as adults.

Violence against Women

The Crime Bill provides for protection of women who are victims of domestic violence and/or stalking. This is the first time a major federal anticrime bill has addressed violence against women and provided strict sanctions against the offender(s).

Other Categories

The Crime Bill includes other important categories. Child abusers, for example, must be registered with local law enforcement for ten years following their release from prison. The Midnight sports component funds organizations providing evening activities for youth (e.g., basketball) in high crime areas.

In the 1996 election year, discussion focused on the increased number of police officers to be hired. Finch (1996) speculates that in its present form, the bill has sufficient funds to hire twenty thousand officers. What impact would this increase have? These "cops on the beat" were expected to function in a community policing capacity. Opponents argued that this was political rhetoric; there was seldom mention of the cost to states to implement and/or supplement the enactment of the bill. Increased law enforcement, it was argued, meant more arrests, prosecutors, correctional officers, and prisons—all of which would require more tax dollars. And after federal funds were depleted at the end of the Crime Bill's six year appropriation period, who would finance the newly-hired officers and programs? Opponents of Crime Bill spending argue the following:

1. Too much pork. The Crime Bill was created not to reduce crime, but to act as a vehicle for spending billions of dollars—a concept linked to former President Nixon.
2. A form of implementing more social programs. The Crime Bill includes a limited number of creative preventive programs; instead, it continues to fund old unsuccessful programs. There is little evidence, for example, that midnight basketball has deterred criminal behavior among high-risk youths.
3. The bill will make taxpayers poorer, not safer. Urban areas already spend to fight crime without seeing real results. Giving cities more money, therefore, will not necessarily decrease crime. To the contrary, crime has increased even in wealthier cities despite federal aid.
4. The federal government should not build state prisons or pay local law enforcement salaries. If the federal government lacks funds, as it claims in its inability to balance the budget, why give the states dollars it does not have?
5. Washington is using the Crime Bill as a distraction. States are competing for these funds; many communities, however, are spending without providing adequate training, and little of the funding is being directed to truly destitute areas. It is likely, therefore, that enormous spending will result in little or minimal crime reduction.

While the Crime Bill has its pros and cons, it offers an opportunity for communities and law enforcement officers to bridge the communication gap and eliminate the stereotypes that have long hindered positive interaction.

Affirmative Action

The term "affirmative action" can be traced back to the National Labor Relations Act (a.k.a. Wagner Act of 1935), one of the first federal laws to focus on labor-management relations by protecting labor's right to organize and bargain (Becker et al. 1982). In 1941, affirmative action emerged again when Franklin D. Roosevelt, concerned that everyone have equal opportunity to work, issued Executive Order 8802 outlawing discrimination in employment policies (Greene 1989). In 1950, a bill on equal employment opportunity introduced in the House of Representatives included the term affirmative action (Burstein 1985, 30).

No President, however, used the term publicly until John F. Kennedy spoke of affirmative action as a means of promoting equal opportunity in Executive Order 1095 (Becker et al. 1982). Lyndon Johnson, then, signed a bill calling for federal contractors to take affirmative action in hiring qualified minorities (Chavez 1998). Johnson went further by issuing Executive Order 11246, establishing affirmative action guidelines that federal contractors were to follow in hiring minorities and women. For the first time, affirmative action's objectives were racially motivated (Sowell 1981).

Affirmative action is designed to equalize the labor market, education, and housing by granting all qualified persons legal access to resources and by making discrimination based on race unlawful. Under the plan, the federal government made available funds for programs aimed at hiring minorities and women. Agencies and organizations could apply for the funding if they demonstrated that they hired qualified personnel. Some companies, however, established a quota system earmarking jobs especially for minorities and women. Others hired unqualified minorities and women to prove them incompetent while receiving federal dollars. Such hiring practices painted minorities and women as incompetent, mere symbols of affirmative action. Some white males even feel anger toward minorities and women for taking jobs away from them.

Affirmative action falls under Title VII of the 1964 Civil Rights Act, a section designed to compensate individuals and groups victimized by discrimination in both the past and present. Debate questions whether affirmative action is the best remedy. It is the responsibility of the U.S. Supreme Court to interpret the Civil Rights law; when hearing cases involving affirmative action, its primary focus should be on Title VII.

President Bush reacted to two Supreme Court cases (*Grutter V. Bollinger* and *Gratz v. Bollinger*) by speaking out against affirmative action. In the cases, the University of Michigan was accused of violating the 14th amendment (equal protection clause) and Title VI of the 1964 Civil Rights Act. In *Gratz v.*

Bollinger, the University admitted using race as a factor in its undergraduate admissions policy so as to ensure a diverse student body. Students were admitted under a quota system in which extra points (twenty out of a maximum of 150) were applied to Native American, Hispanic, and African American applicants—a practice the Court ruled unconstitutional. In *Grutter v. Bollinger*, the Court considered the University of Michigan law school's use of racial preference in their admissions policy. In reviewing each applicant, the admissions committee considered all factors, including race. In a five to four decision, the Court ruled the admissions policy constitutional, as minority applicants suffered no undue harm (New York Times 2003).

One of the more notable cases, the *Regents of the University of California v. Bakke* (1978), addressed affirmative action in schools. When Allan P. Bakke, a white male, claimed that he had been denied admission to the medical school because of the minority quota system, the Supreme Court ruled the quota system unconstitutional because of discrimination against whites. It should be noted that in this decision, the Court did allow the constitutionality of plans favoring minorities (Chavez 1998).

A landmark case, *Adarand v. Pena* (1995), examined the federal government's authority to implement affirmative action programs. In 1989, Adarand, a white owner of a Colorado construction company, made a sub-contractor's bid for a guardrail construction contract with the Department of Transportation. While Adarand submitted the lowest bid, the contract went to a Hispanic (Gonzales) company. Adarand sued, claiming that minority preference had violated his Fifth Amendment right to equal protection under the law. In a five-four decision, the Supreme Court ruled that "all racial classifications imposed by whatever federal, state, or local governmental actor, must be analyzed by a reviewing court under strict scrutiny" (Rosen 1996, 21).

Those opposing affirmative action as a race quote system applauded the decision, but felt that the court did not go far enough. Still, the decision was considered a start to the elimination of programs offering preferential treatment to minorities and women (Gest 1995). Many in favor of affirmative action suggest that the policy made it possible for minorities and women to enter some fields (e.g., law enforcement) in administrative capacities. The Reverend Jesse Jackson has questioned whether female or African American justices would be sitting on the Supreme Court had there been no affirmative action.

The Crime Bill and affirmative action will continue to be debated; their implications are great to the future of American society. For the law enforcement officer, despite his feelings on the issues, it is important to maintain professionalism and use the law in decision-making.

Toward Improving Police-Minority Relationships

Conflict and stress has long existed between minorities and police officers. The task today is to improve this relationship. Because the burden of proof is on the officer, specific recommendations are delineated; many are not new, but consideration is given to those agencies that have community policing components incorporated into their organizations, and to those involved in community and problem-oriented policing.

Police officers should strive for more positive interaction with minorities. While most interactions have been negative, officers should not consider all minority suspects criminals. To the contrary, they should treat minority suspects as they would want members of their own family treated. Opponents claim that the job allows little time to "relate." While these two concepts are often discussed separately, they are in fact interrelated—when an officer is "policing," interaction is part of the job.

Interaction should be continually monitored. While such monitoring is usually received negatively, it would fill a gap identified by the National Officers of Black Law Enforcement Executives (NOBLE) by providing community policing or police-community relationship programs with an evaluation component. Without such evaluation, NOBLE claims, accurate assessments of community oriented policing are difficult because success or failure is based on crime reduction rates, often a misleading figure. Evaluations can be formal or informal, and should occur at different levels: intra-organizationally, community, and individually.

Intra-organizational evaluations occur when the organization rates its own performance. While many police organizations already perform such evaluations, they either fail to rate how the organization interacts with citizens, or claim to have addressed issues of diversity in seminars. The seminars, however, are sporadic, and largely superficial—top administrators are not required to attend, and officers are not able to discuss situations relevant to them (e.g., handling situations where the officer becomes the minority).

Community evaluations are fairly informal; the community tells the police how they are doing. Some policing units allow residents to complete surveys, offer suggestions at community substations, and meet periodically to provide feedback. Those programs receiving federal funds specifically for the implementation of community policing should have to explain the methods used in obtaining such evaluations.

Although individual job performance evaluations are expected, they are often ignored; many officers consider such evaluations superficial, providing limited feedback on actual performance. The same limitation applies to supervisor evaluations—as few are involved in direct supervision, evaluations are based primarily on arrest rates, citations, and the number of cases closed. Seldom is there discussion on their interaction with citizens.

Police organizations and criminal justice programs should have more open discussions on diversity. Students, however, often resist because they believe that:

1. Such discussions might further the gap between majority and minority;
2. Discrimination today is limited to those who are incompetent; if the citizen is qualified, he should have no problem getting a job or an education;
3. Past atrocities have no bearing on the current situation ("I did not enslave blacks so why are they so angry with me"); and
4. They can avoid problems by treating everyone the same, ignoring that such a practice might exacerbate the problem by ignoring that people are unique. Perhaps the goal should be to treat everyone with respect, learn from others, and admit mistakes.

When exploring positive interactions between police officers and minorities, discussion is often limited to white officers policing minority communities, the homosexual community, or the elderly population. Culturally matching officers has advantages and disadvantages. Oftentimes, minority officers are placed in minority communities assuming that they will interact well with their own population. According to Cox & Fitzgerald (1996), however, this can create problems because:

1. Minority officers are stricter with their own race, some considering them traitors;
2. Limiting officers to policing only their own racial group prevents their learning how to interact with people different to themselves; and
3. These officers might be considered not competent enough to police all citizens.

Law enforcement officers must remain abreast of current research in the field of genetics, because a new kind of racist criminal may be emerging. Jaimes (1995) explains that this occurs when patients, designated as medical research participants, are subjected to bizarre treatment methods (not approved by health authorities) in order to find cures for terminal illnesses, or to offer proof of human cloning in the quest to create "designer babies." Because these projects are covert, the patient or patient's family is left unaware of the research goals.

Guyot (1991) calls for "fairness" in law enforcement in order to provide better services and improve individual performance. Fairness, however, is based on personal prejudices. If police organizations are allowed to function primarily on the basis of what they consider fair, their ideas will be influenced by personal experiences, and will likely stereotype minorities. This could result in an escalation of discriminatory practices.

Even in organized civilizations such as the Greek and Roman Empire, life has never been fair—not in homes where decisions are made based on favoritism, not in the court system where decisions are made based on socioeconomic status, and not in academia where some students receive high acclimates for creativity while others receive negative feedback. Why, then, should we expect fairness from law enforcement officers? Perhaps what we can expect is professional behavior, respect for each citizen, and performance based on law rather than personal biases.

In 2002-03, the Supreme Court interpreted the following major laws that will certainly impact the criminal justice system:

1. Affirmative action. *Grutter v. Bollinger* upheld the University of Michigan's admission policies that consider race a factor; *Gratz v. Bollinger*, however, rejected the use of a quota system.
2. Sodomy. *Lawrence v. Texas* (a six to three decision) determined that laws criminalizing gay sex violate civil rights.
3. Internet filters at libraries. *United States v. American Library Association* (a six to three decision) made it such that libraries will lose federal funding if they do not install pornography filters.
4. California Three Strikes laws. *Ewing v. California* and *Lockyer v. Andrade* (a five to four decision) determined that life sentencing laws for third felonies are constitutional.
5. Megan's Laws. *Smith v. Doe* (six to three decision) and *Connecticut Department of Public Safety v. Doe* (unanimous decision) determined that laws requiring sex offenders to register with the state are constitutional.
6. Cross Burning. *Virginia v. Black* (a six to three decision) determined that cross burning overshadows free speech as an instrument of racial terror; states, therefore, can punish violators.
7. Abortion Protester. *Scheidler v. NOW* and *Operation Rescue v. NOW* (eight to one decision) established that federal racketeering and extortion laws cannot be used to prevent protesting of abortion clinics.
8. Copyright extension. *Eldred v. Ashcroft* (a seven to two decision) upheld a twenty-year extension to keep copyrighted material out of the public domain.
9. Prescription drugs. *Pharmaceutical Research v. Concanon* (a six to three decision) determined that states can force lower prescription prices.

The USA Patriot Act of 2001 has changed policing in society, creating debate among civil rights organizations and citizens over the increased powers given to law enforcement officers (especially regarding surveillance and investigative authority). Some, such as the ACLU, argue that law enforcement organizations have too much unchecked power—pen registers (monitor outgoing phone numbers), tap and trace (monitor incoming phone numbers), and access to financial and student records threaten citizens' rights. For the first time, in January 2004, Los Angeles federal judge Audrey Collins struck down part of the act that bars "expert advise and assistance" to foreign terrorist groups as unconstitutional (1st and 5th amendment violations) (Whitcomb 2004). More court challenges are expected before 2005, when Congress considers changes to the act.

Summary

Law enforcement in America has experienced drastic changes with the passage of the Crime Bill and the USA Patriot Act. While police officers have been granted extensive powers to combat terrorism, concerns remain about the protection of civil liberties. In all likelihood, given the raised alert status, officers will continue to be expected to protect homeland security, while also protecting and serving the citizens—all while their increased powers are questioned.

As society becomes more diverse, so does the need for criminal justice students to discuss related issues. These issues are not simply political topics that will resolve themselves—rather, they must be continuously discussed in order to sensitize students to the need to protect individual rights during times of distress.

Key Concepts

Adarand v. Pena	Three Strikes
Affirmative Action	Title VII (Civil Rights Act)
Crime Bill	*University of California v. Bakke*
NOBLE	Wagner Act 1935

Questions for Discussion

1. Explain the impact of the Crime Bill on policing. How has it helped your community?

2. Affirmative action is an issue that continues to cause much debate. What is it and how has it impacted America?

3. According to the U.S. Constitution, all individuals are granted equal protection under the law. Discuss how your community provides equal protection for its citizens.

4. What are some methods used in your community to improve race relations between minorities and the police?

5. Discuss methods of ensuring equal opportunity for all qualified citizens seeking employment regardless of race, religion, gender, or sexual preference. What is meant by race conscious decision making (as in the University of Michigan decisions)?

Suggested Reading

<www.afda.org/afda/key/94bill.htm>. An overview of the 1994 Federal Crime Bill.

<www.affirmativeaction.org>. American Association for Affirmative Action.

<www.eeoc.gov/policy/vii.html>. The purpose and an in-depth look at Title VII of the Civil Rights Act of 1964.

REFERENCES

AARP. n.d. Overview: AARP History. <http://www.aarp.org/about_aarp/ aarp_overview/ a2003-01-13-aarphistory.html>.

Adam, B.D. 1995. *The Rise of a Gay and Lesbian Movement.* New York, NY: Twayne Publishers, Prentice Hall International.

Adarand v. Pena, 000 U.S. U10252 (1995)

Adler, F., Mueller, G., & Laufer, W. 1996. *Criminal Justice: The Core.* New York, NY: McGraw-Hill Companies.

Aiken, L. 1995. *Aging: An Introduction to Gerontology.* Belmont, CA: Sage Publications.

Alex, N. 1969. *Black in Blue.* Englewood Cliffs, NJ: Prentice Hall.

Alexander, W. 1888. *History of the Colored Race in America.* Kansas City, MO: Palmetto Publisher Company.

Allen, H., & Simonsen C. 1995. *Corrections in America.* Englewood Cliffs, NJ: Prentice-Hall.

Altman, D. 1982. *The Homosexualization of America.* New York, NY: St. Martin's Press.

American Demographics. 2002. *Progress in Education* 24 (10). American Demographics Analysis of Census 2000 Data, U.S. Census Bureau. Washington, DC: U.S. Census Bureau, Dept. of Commerce.

Anonymous. 2002. *Through Our Enemies' Eyes: Osama bin Laden, Radical Islam, and the Future of America.* Washington, DC: Brassey's, Inc.

Anthias, F. 1990. Race and class revisited: Conceptualizing race and racism. *The Sociological Review 38* (1), 19–42.

Aswad, B.C. 2003. Arab americans. In R. Scupin (Ed.), *Race and Ethnicity: An Anthropological Focus on the United States and the World.* Upper Saddle River, NJ: Prentice Hall.

Axtell, J. 1981. *The European and the Indian: Essays in the Ethnohistory of Colonial North America.* Oxford, NY: Oxford University Press.

Becker, G.S., Sowell, T., Vonnegut, K., Block, W., Walker, M. 1982. *Discrimination, Affirmative Action, and Equal Opportunity: An Economic and Social Perspective.* Vancouver, B.C., Canada: Fraser Institute.

Benson, J. 2003. Asian americans. In R. Scupin (Ed.), *Race and Ethnicity: An Anthropological Focus on the United States and the World.* Upper River Saddle, NJ: Prentice Hall.

Bergen, P. 2001. *Holy War, Inc.: Inside the Secret World of Osama bin Laden.* New York, NY: The Free Press.

Berlet, C. 1995. Armed Militias, Right Wing Populism, & Scapegoating. Political Research Associates. <http://www.etext.org/Politics/Arm.The.Spirit/Antifa/militias.berlet>.

Bernstein, R., & Bergman, M. 2003. Hispanic Population Reaches All-Time High of 38.8 Million, New Census Bureau Estimates Show. <http://www.census.gov/Press-Release/www/2003/cb03-100.html>.

Bhungalia, L. 2001. Native american women and violence. *National NOW Times,* Spring issue. <http://now.org/nnt/spring-2001/nativeamerican.html>.

Bigler, E. 2003. Hispanic americans/latinos. In R. Scupin (Ed.), *Race and Ethnicity: An Anthropological Focus on the United States and the World.* Upper Saddle River, NJ: Prentice Hall.

Birzer, M.L., & Tannehill, R. 2001. A more effective training approach for contemporary policing. *Police Quarterly* 4(2), 233–52.

Blumenfeld, W., & Raymond, D. 1993. *Looking at Gay and Lesbian Life.* Boston, MA: Beacon Press.

Bodrero, D. 2002. Law enforcement's new challenge to investigate, interdict, & prevent terrorism. *The Police Chief* (February), 41–48.

Bonney, R. 2003. American indians. In R. Scupin (Ed.), *Race and Ethnicity: An Anthropological Focus on the United States and the World.* Upper Saddle River, NJ: Prentice Hall.

Bowers v. Hardwick, 478 U.S. 186 (1986)

Brace, C.L. 2000. Does Race Exist? An Antagonist's Perspective. <www.pbs.org/wgbh/nova/first/brace.html>.

Brillon, Y. 1987. *Victimization and Fear of Crime Among the Elderly.* Toronto, Canada: Butterworths Legal Publishing Company.

Brown v. Board of Education, 347 U.S. 483 (1954)

Brown, D. 2003. Ethnicity and ethnocentrism: Are they natural? In R. Scupin (Ed.), *Race and Ethnicity: An Anthropological Focus on the United States and the World.* Upper Saddle River, NJ: Prentice Hall.

Brown, S. 2003. African americans. In R. Scupin (Ed.), *Race and Ethnicity: An Anthropological Focus on the United States and the World.* Upper Saddle River, New Jersey: Prentice Hall.

Brown, U.M. 2001. *The Interracial Experience: Growing Up Black/White Racially Mixed in the United States.* Westport, CA: Praeger Publishers.

Buffalohead, W. 1996. Reflections on native american cultural rights and resources. In M. Rodgers (Ed.), *Multiculturalism Experiences, Multiculturalism Theories*. New York, NY: McGraw Hill Publishers.

Bumiller, E. 2003. Saddam Deadline is Today. *The Daily Reflector*. North Carolina. March 19, page 1.

Burstein, P. 1985. *Discrimination, Jobs, and Politics: The Struggle for Equal Employment Opportunity in the United States Since the New Deal*. Chicago, IL: University of Chicago Press.

Burton, A. 1996. Frontier Indian Police. <www.coax.net/people/lwf/fip_pt1. htm>. Trotwood, OH: LWF Publications.

Bush, M.L. 2000. *Servitude in Modern Times*. Malden, MA: Blackwell Publishers Inc.

Bushnell, G.H.S. 1986. *The First Americans*. New York, NY: McGraw Hill Publishers.

Cafferty, P., & Engstrom, D. 2000. *Hispanics in the United States*. New Brunswick, NJ: Transaction Books.

Capozzoli, T.K. & McVey, R.S. 2000. *Kids Killing Kids: Managing Violence and Gangs in Schools*. Baca Raton, FL: St. Lucie Press.

Caron, S.L. 1998. *Cross-cultural Perspectives on Human Sexuality*. Needham Heights, MA: Allyn & Bacon.

Case, S., Brett, P., & Foster, S.L. 1995. *Cruising the Performative: Interventions into the Representation of Ethnicity, Nationality, and Sexuality*. Bloomington, IN: Indiana University Press.

CBS News. 2003. Bush Signs Medicare Bill. <http://www.cbsnews.com/stories/2003/10/ 23/politics/main579645.shtml>.

The Centre for National Security Studies. 2004. Recent Trends in Domestic and International Terrorism. <http://nsi.org/Library/Terrorism/tertrend. html>.

Chalmers, D. 1965. *Hooded Americanism*. Garden City, NY: Doubleday & Company.

Charrad, M.M. 1998. Cultural diversity within islam: Veils and laws in tunisia. In H.L. Bodman & N. Tohidi (Eds.), *Women in Muslim Societies: Diversity Within Unity* (pp. 63–79). Boulder, CO: Lynne Rienner.

Chavez, L. 1998. *The Color Bind: California's Battle to End Affirmative Action*. Berkeley, CA: University of California Press.

Chen, G. 1995. Differences in self-disclosure patterns among americans versus chinese: A comparative study. *Journal of Cross-Cultural Psychology, 26*(1).

Cherokee v. Georgia, 30 U.S. 1 (1831)

Chuman, F.F. 1976. *The Bamboo People: The Law and Japanese-Americans*. Del Mar, CA: Publisher's Inc.

CNN 1996. Negotiator: No one coming out of freeman compound. <http://www.cnn.com/US/9605/01/freemen.4pm/>.

Cole, G., & Smith, C. 2005. *Criminal Justice in America* (4th ed.). Belmont, CA: Wadsworth Thomson Learning.

Combs, C. 2000. *Terrorism in the Twenty-first Century* (2nd ed.). Upper Saddle River, NJ: Prentice Hall.

Connecticut Department of Public Safety v. Doe, 000 U.S. 01-1231 (2003)

Cordesman, A.H. 2002. *Terrorism, Asymmetric Warfare, and Weapons of Mass Destruction: Defending the U.S. Homeland.* Westport, CT: Praeger Publishing.

Covert Action Quarterly 1995, Spring. Militias. <http://www.logicsouth.com/~lcoble/ conspire/caq.txt>.

Cox, S.M. & Fitzgerald, J.D. 1996. *Police in Community Relations: Critical Issues* (3rd ed.). Madison, WI: Brown & Benchmark.

Coyle, A., & Kitzinger, C. 2000. *Lesbian and Gay Psychology.* Oxford, UK: Blackwell Pub.

Cruikshank, M. 1992. *The Gay and Lesbian Liberation Movement.* New York, NY: Routledge, Chapman & Hall, Inc.

Dailey, N. 1998. *When Baby Boom Women Retire.* Westport, CT: Praeger Pub.

Daniel, G.R. 2002. *More than Black? Multiracial Identity and the New Racial Order.* PA: Temple University Press.

Daniels, D. 2002. *Remarks.* Assistant Attorney General. Office of Justice Programs at the Hispanic American Police Command Officers Association's 29th Annual Training Conference in Albuquerque, New Mexico.

DATA. 2003. *The Brown University Digest of Addiction: Theory and Application, 22* (5).

Dickerson v. U.S., 530 U.S. 428 (2000)

Dinnerstein, L., Nichols, R.L., & Reimers, D.M. 1990. *Natives and Strangers.* New York, NY: Oxford University Press.

Dover, B., & Dover, K.J. 1978. *Greek Homosexuality.* London: Unwin Brothers Ltd.

Dulaney, W. 1996. *Black Police in America.* Bloomington, IN: Indian University Press.

Eldred v. Ashcroft, 000 U.S. 01-618 (2003)

Eltis, D. 2000. *The Rise of African Slavery in the Americas.* New York, NY: Cambridge University Press.

Emerson, S. 2002. *American Jihad: The Terrorists Living Among Us.* New York, NY: Free Press.

Ewing v. California, 000 U.S. 01-6978 (2003)

Fernandez, C. 1995. Testimony of the association of multiethnic americans before the subcommittee on census, statistics, and postal personnel of the u.s. house of representatives. In N. Zack (Ed.), *American Mixed Race*. Lanham, MD: Rowman & Littlefield Publishers.

Flowers, R. 1988. *Minorities and Criminality*. New York, NY: Greenwood Press.

Foley, D., & Moss, K. 2001. *Cultural Diversity in the United States*. Maulden, MA: Blackwell Publishing.

Frazier, T.R. 1988. *Afro American History*. Chicago, IL: Dorsey Press.

Frontline. 1998. The Kevorkian Verdict: The Thanatron. <http://www.pbs.org/wgbh/pages/frontline/kevorkian/aboutk/thanatronblurb.html>.

Galliher, J.F. 1989. *Criminology: Human Rights, Criminal Law, and Crime*. Englewood Cliffs, NJ: Prentice-Hall.

Ganor, B. 2003. Defining terrorist: Is one man's terrorist another man's freedom fighter? In T.J. Badey (Ed.), *Violence and Terrorism* (6th ed.). Guilford, CT: McGraw-Hill/Dushkin.

Garrett, M.T., & Carroll, J.J. 2000. Mending the broken circle: Treatment of substance dependence among Native Americans. *Journal of Counseling & Development, 78*(4), 379–389.

Gauthier, J.G. 2002. *Measuring America: The Decennial Censuses From 1970 to 2000*. <http://www.census.gov/prod/2002pubs/pol02marv-pt1.pdf>.

Gelfand, D. 1994. *Aging and Ethnicity*. New York, NY: Springer Publishing Company.

Gibson, R.C. 1987. Defining retirement for black Americans. In D.E. Gelfand & C. Barresi (Eds.), *Ethnicity and Aging* (pp. 224–238). New York, NY: Springer Publishing Company.

Goldberg, D. 1994. *Multiculturalism*. Cambridge, MA: Blackwell Publisher.

Goldberg, D. 1995. Made in the u.s.a.: Racial mixing n' matching. In N. Zack (Ed.), *American Mixed Race*. Lanham, MD: Rowman & Littlefield.

Goldstein, H. 1990. *Problem-Oriented Policing*. New York, NY: McGraw-Hill.

Goldstein, A.P, & Huff, C.R. 1993. *The Gang Intervention Handbook*. Champaign, IL: Research Press.

Gonzalez, J. 2000. *Harvest the Empire*. New York, NY: Viking Press.

Gonzales, M. 1999. The chicano movement 1965–1975. In M. Gonzales (Ed.), *Mexicanos: A History of Mexicans in the United States*. Bloomington, IN: Indiana University Press.

Goode, J. 2001. Against Cultural Essentism. *Cultural Diversity in the United States*. Maulden, MA: Blackwell Publishing.

Goodridge v. Department of Public Health, 798 NE2d 941 (Mass 2003)

Gratz v. Bollinger, 000 U.S. 02-516 (2003)

Greenbaum, P. 1985. Non-verbal differences in communication style between american indian and anglo classrooms. *American Education Research Journal, 22*(1), 101–115.

Greene, K. 1989. *Affirmative Action and Principles of Justice.* New York, NY: Greenwood Press.

Grieco, L.M., & Cassidy, R.C. 2001. *Overview of Race and Hispanic origin: Census 2000 Brief.* Washington, DC: U.S. Department of Commerce Economics and Statistics Administration.

Grutter v. Bollinger, 000 U.S. 02-241 (2003)

Guyot, D. 1991. *Policing as though People Matter.* Philadelphia, PA: Temple University Press.

Guzman, B. 2001. *The Hispanic Population: Census 2000 Brief.* Washington, DC: U.S. Department of Commerce Economics and Statistics Administration.

Haberfeld, M.R. 2002. *Critical Issues in Police Training.* Upper Saddle River, NJ: Prentice Hall.

Hamm, M. 1993. *American Skinheads: The Criminology and Control of Hate Crimes.* Westport, CT: Praeger Series in Criminology and Crime Control Policy.

Harmer, H. 2001. *Slavery, Emancipation and Civil Rights.* New York, NY: Pearson Education Limited.

Harris, D.A. (Ed.) 1995. *Multiculturalism from the Margins: Non-Dominant Voices on Difference and Diversity.* Westport, CT: Bergin & Garvey.

Hartman-Stein, P.E. 1999. Training for psychologists in aging would get boost if senate bill passes. *National Psychologist, 8*(5), 8.

Hess, K., & Wrobleski, H. 1993. *Police Operations.* St. Paul, MN: West Publishing Company.

Hickman, M. 2003. *Tribal Law Enforcement, 2000.* Fact Sheet. Washington, DC: U.S. Department of Justice, Office of Justice Programs, Bureau of Justice Statistics.

Hobbs, F.B. & Damon, B.L. 1996. *65+ in the United States.* U.S. Census Bureau, P23–190 Current Population Reports: Special Studies. <http://www.census.gov/prod/1/pop/ p23-190.html>.

Hoffman, J. 2000. Special report: Police corps—An update two years after the first police corps graduation. *Law and Order, 48*(1), 50–58.

Human Rights Watch 2002. The September 11 Backlash. <http://www.hrw.org/reports/ 2002/usahate.usa1102-04.htm>.

International Association of Chiefs of Police. 1998. *The Future of Women in Policing: Mandates for Action.* Alexandria, VA.

Jackson, M.S. 2003. Law Enforcement's Response to Illegal Street Gang Activity. In A.R. Roberts (Ed.), *Critical Issues in Crime and Justice.* Thousand Oaks, CA: Sage Publications.

Jackson, M.S. 1989. Juvenile gangs: Analyzing the problem. In W. Hemmons (Ed.), *The State of Black Cleveland.* Cleveland, OH: Urban League of Cleveland.

Jacobson, D. 1984. Indians of North America. *The New Book of Knowledge.* Toronto, Canada: Grolier, Inc.

Jaimes, M. 1995. Some kind of indian. In N. Zack (Ed.), *American Mixed Race.* Lanham, MD: Rowman & Littlefield Publishers.

Jehl, D. 2005. Pentagon seeks to transfer more detainees from base in cuba. *New York Times.* <www.nytimes.com/2005/03/11/politics/11detain.html? pagewanted=1>.

Jenness, V., & Broad, K. 1997. *Hate Crimes: New Social Movements and the Politics of Violence.* New York, NY: Aldine de Gruyter Publisher.

Jensen, A. 1998. *The g Factor: The Science of Mental Ability.* Westport, CT: Praeger Publisher.

Jones, N., & Smith, A.S. 2001. The Two or More Races Population: 2000. *Census 2000 Brief.* Washington, DC: U.S. Census Bureau.

Josephy, A.M. 1991. *The Indian Heritage of America* (Rev. ed.). Boston, MA: Houghton Mifflin Company.

Kaysen, C., Miller, S., Malin, M., Norahaus, W., & Steinbruner, J. 2002. *War With Iraq: Costs, Consequences and Alternatives.* Cambridge, MA: American Academy of Arts & Sciences.

Kennedy, K.R. 1995. But professor, why teach race identification if races don't exist? *Journal of Forensic Science, 40*(5), 797–800.

Kitano, H., & Daniels, R. 2001. *Asian Americans: Emerging Minorities* (3rd ed.). Englewood Cliffs, NY: Prentice-Hall.

Kitano, H., & Daniels, R. 1988. *Asian Americans: Emerging Minorities.* Englewood, NJ: Prentice Hall.

Klockars, C. 1985. *The Idea of Police.* Beverly Hills, CA: Sage Publications.

Knapp, D. 1996. Freemen May Meet With State Officials. <http://cnn.com/ US/9604/30/ freemen.am/>.

Knox, G.W. 2000. A national assessment of gangs and security threat groups (STGs) in adult correctional institutions: Results of the 1999 adult corrections survey. *Journal of Gang Research, 7*(3), 1–45.

Kochman Group LLC. 1993. Adapted from Kochman's Communication Consultants Participants' Manual. July Juvenile Court Training Cultural Diversity Training.

Krane, J. 1999. The Graying of America's Prisons: An Emerging Corrections Crisis. <http://www.angelfire.com/la/kaylee/prison/html>.

Kupperman, R.H., & Smith, D.M. 1993. Coping with biological terrorism. In B. Roberts (Ed.), *Biological Weapons: Weapons of the Future?* Washington, DC: Center for Strategic and International Studies.

Lamphere, L. 2001. Understanding united states diversity: Where do we go? In T.C. Patterson & I. Susser (Eds.), *Cultural Diversity in the United States*. Maulden, MA: Blackwell Publishing.

Langworthy, R.H., & Travis, L.F. 1994. *Policing in America: A Balance of Forces*. New York, NY: MacMillan Publishing.

Laqueur, W. 1999. *The New Terrorism Fanaticism and the Arms of Mass Destruction*. New York, NY: Oxford University Press.

Lawrence v. Texas, 000 U.S. 02-102 (2003)

Leinen, S. 1984. *Black Police, White Society*. New York, NY: New York University Press.

Lieberman, E.S. 2003. *Race and Regionalism in the Politics of Taxation in Brazil and South Africa*. New York, NY: Cambridge University Press.

Lien, P. 2001. *The Making of Asian American Through Political Participation*. Philadelphia, PA: Temple University Press.

Lockyer v. Andrade, 000 U.S. 01-1127 (2003)

Locust, C. 1990. Wounding the spirit: Discrimination and traditional american indian belief systems. In G. Thomas (Ed.), *U.S. Race Relations in the 1980s and 1990s*. Thomas. New York, NY: Hemisphere Publishers.

Locust, C. 1996. Unpublished commentary comments.

Long, G. 1993. Homosexual relationships in a unique setting: The male prison. In L. Diamant (Ed.), *Homosexual Issues in the Workplace*. Washington, DC: Taylor & Francis Publishers.

Long, R.E. 1997. *Multiculturalism*. New York, NY: W. Wilson, Co.

Maas, P. 1996, May 19. "Can John Magaw save the ATF?" Parade Magazine.

MacEachern, S. 2003. The concept of race in anthropology. In R. Scupin (Ed.), *Race and Ethnicity: An Anthropological Focus on the United States and the World*. Upper Saddle, NJ: Prentice Hall.

Mailman, S. 1995. California's proposition 187 and its lessons. *New York Law Journal*, Col.1: 3.

Mann, C.R. 1993. *Unequal Justice: A Question of Color*. Bloomington, IN: Indiana University Press.

Marger, M. 1994. *Race and Ethnic Relations*. Belmont, CA: Wadsworth Publishing Company.

Martin, S. 1989. Female officers on the move? A status report on women in policing. In R.G. Dunham & G.P. Alpert (Eds.), *Critical Issues in Policing: Contemporary Reading*. Prospect Heights, IL: Waveland Press.

Martin, S. 1991. The effectiveness of affirmative action. *Justice Quarterly*, 8(4), 489–504.

Maxson, C.L., Whitlock, M.L., & Klein, M.W. 1998. Vulnerability to street gang membership: Implications for practice. *Social Service Review*, 72(1), 70–91.

Mays, V.M., Ponce, N.A., Washington, D.L., & Cochran, S.D. 2003. Classification of race and ethnicity: Implications for public health. *Annual Review of Public Health, 24,* 83–110.

McCartney, J.T. 1992. *Black Power Ideologies.* Philadelphia, PA: Temple University Press.

McKinnon, J. 2001. *The Black Population: 2000.* Washington, DC: U.S. Department of Commerce Economics and Statistics Administration.

McVey, P. 1997. *Terrorism and Local Law Enforcement: A Multidimensional Challenge for the Twenty-first Century.* Springfield, IL: Charles Thomas.

Miller, L., & Hess, K. 1994. *Community Policing.* St. Paul, MN: West Publishing Company.

Miller, N. 1995. *Out of the Past: Gay and Lesbian History from 1869 to the Present.* New York, NY: Vintage Books.

Min, P.G. 1995. *Asian Americans.* Thousand Oaks, London, New Delhi: Sage Publications.

Mintz, S. 2003. *Digital History.* <www.digitalhistory.uh.edu> and The Library of Congress website: <www.loc.gov>, <www.memory.loc.gov/features/immig/alt/timeline.html#>.

Miranda v. Arizona, 384 U.S. 436 (1966)

Montagu, A. 1997. *Man's Most Dangerous Myth: The Fallacy of Race* (6th ed.). New York, NY: Columbia University Press.

Moore, R. 2003. *The Hunt for Bin Laden.* New York, NY: Random House.

Morison, S.E. 1974. *The European Discovery of America: The Southern Voyages A.D. 1492–1616.* New York, NY: Oxford University Press.

Morton v. Mancari, 417 U.S. 535 (1974)

Mullins, W. 1988. *Terrorist Organizations in the United States.* Springfield, IL: Charles C. Thomas Publisher.

Murray, C., & Herrinstein, R. 1994. *The Bell Curve: Intelligence & Class Structure in American Life.* New York, NY: Free Press.

Myers, G.E. 1995. *A Municipal Mother.* Corvallis, OR: Oregon State University Press.

Myrdal, G. 1944. *The American Dilemma.* New York, NY: Harper & Brothers.

National Institute of Justice. *Crime and Justice Research: American Indian & Alaska Native Issues.* U.S. Department of Justice. Office of Justice Programs. <www.ncjrs.org/pdffiles1/nij/s1000455.pdf>.

The New Book of Knowledge. 1984. New York, NY: Random House.

Newton, D.E. & Risch, S.J. 1981. Homosexuality and education: A review of the issue. *The High School Journal, 64,* 191–202.

Newton, M. 2001. *The Invisible Empire: The Ku Klux Klan in Florida.* Gainseville, FL: UP of Florida.

Nishi, S. 1995. Japanese Americans. In P.G. Min (Ed.), *Asian Americans*. Thousand Oaks, CA: Sage Publications.

Nydell, M. 1987. *Understanding Arabs: A Guide for Westerners*. Yarmouth, ME: Intercultural Press, Inc.

Office of Homeland Security. 2002. *National Strategy for Homeland Security*. Washington, DC: Office of Homeland Security.

Office of the Police Corps and Law Enforcement Education. 2000. *The Police Corps: Guidelines for Training*. Washington, DC: Office of Justice Programs, U.S. Department of Justice.

Office of the Police Corps and Law Enforcement Education. 2001. *The Police Corps: Some Brief Descriptions*. Washington, DC: Office of Justice Programs, U.S. Department of Justice.

Ogunwole, S. 2002. The American Indian and Alaska native population: 2000. *U.S. Census 2000*. Washington, DC: U.S. Department of Commerce Economics and Statistics Administration.

Pearson, H. 1994. *The Shadow of a Panther*. Reading, MA: Addison-Wesley Publishing Company.

People v. Simpson, No. BA097211 (Cal. Super. Ct. L.A. County 1995)

Peter, J. 2004. *Massachusetts High Court Rules Gay Couples Entitled to Marriage*. The Daily Reflector. Greenville, NC: The Associated Press.

Pinkney, A. 1994. *White Hate Crimes*. Chicago, IL: Third World Press.

Plessy v. Ferguson, 163 U.S. 537 (1896)

Powell, C. (Speaker). 2003. U.S. Secretary of State Colin Powell Addresses the U.N. Security Council. <www.whitehouse.gov/news/releases/2003/02/20030205-1.html>.

Prussel, D., & Lonsway, K. 2001. Recruiting women police officers. *Law and Order, 49*(7), 91–96.

Radelet, L.A. 1986. *The Police and the Community* (4th ed.). New York: Macmillan.

Reaves, B., & Hickman, M.J. 2002. Police Departments in Large Cities, 1999–2000. *Bureau of Justice Statistics* Special Report.

Reyhner, J. 1991. The challenge of teaching minority students: An american indian example. *Teaching Education, 4*(1), 103–111.

Riekse, R., & Holstege, H. 1996. *Growing Older in America*. New York, NY: McGraw Hill Publishing Companies.

Roberg, R., & Kuykendall, J. 1990. *Police Organization and Management: Behavior, Theory, and Processes*. Pacific Grove, CA: Brooks/Cole Publishing Company.

Roberg, R., & KuyKendall, J. 1993. *Police and Society*. Belmont, CA: Wadsworth Publishing Company.

Romer v. Evans, 000 U.S. U10179 (1996)

Roots, C.R. 1998. *The Sandwich Generation: Adult Children Caring for Aging Parents.* New York, NY: Garland Publishing.

Rosen, J. 1996, April 22. The day the quotas died: Affirmative action's posthumous life. *The New Republic,* 17, 21.

Rosenblatt, R. (n.d.). Sourcebook. National Academy of Social Insurance. <http://www.nsai.org/publications3901/publications.htm>.

Rushton, J.P. 1999. *Race, Evolution, and Behavior* (sp. abr. ed.). Brunswick, NJ: Transaction Press.

Sauer, C.O. 1971. *Sixteenth-Century North America: The Land and the People as seen by the Europeans.* Berkeley, CA: University of California Press.

Schaie, K.W. & Willis, S.L. 1991. *Adult Development and Aging* (3rd ed.). New York, NY: HarperCollins.

Scheidler v. National Organization for Women, Inc.(NOW), 000 U.S. 01-1118 (2003)

Schlesinger, B., & Schlesinger, R. 1988. *Abuse of the Elderly.* Toronto, Canada: University of Toronto Press.

Scott, J.P. 2001. *Age Through Ethnic Lenses: Caring for the Elderly in a Multicultural Society.* New York, NY: Rowman and Littlefield.

Scott, W. 1986. Attachment to indian culture and the difficult situation: A study of american indian college students. *Youth and Society, 17*(4), 381–95.

Scupin, R. 2003. Ethnicity. In R. Scupin (Ed.), *Race and Ethnicity: An Anthropological Focus on the United States and the World.* Upper Saddle River, NJ: Prentice Hall.

Segal, U. 2002. *A Framework for Immigration: Asians in the United States.* New York, NY: Columbia UP.

Seidman, S. 1996. *Queer Theory/Sociology.* Cambridge, MA: Blackwell.

Senna, J. & Siegel, L.J. 2001. *Essentials of Criminal Justice.* Belmont, CA: Hoover Institute Press.

Shapiro, C. 1998. LaBodega de la Familia: Reaching Out to the Forgotten Victims of Substance Abuse. *Bureau of Justice Assistance Bulletin.* <http://www.ncjrs.org/ pdffiles170595.pdf>.

Sherman, L. 1973. Psychological view of women in policing. *Journal of Police Science and Administration, 1,* 383–94.

Sherman, L. 1975. Evaluation of policewomen on patrol in a suburban police department. *Journal of Police Science & Administration, 3,* 434–38.

Sherman, L. 1978. *Scandal and Reform: Controlling Police Corruption.* Berkeley, CA: University of California Press.

Shockley, W., & Pearson, R. 1992. *Shockley on Eugenics and Race: The Application of Science to the Solution of Human Problems*. Washington, DC: Scott Townsend Publisher.

Shusta, R., Levine, D., Harris, P., & Wong, H. 1995, 2001. *Multicultural Law Enforcement* (2nd ed.). Englewood Cliffs, NJ: Prentice Hall Publishers.

Siasoco, R.V. 1999. Defining hate crimes: No longer a black and white issue. <http:// www.infoplease.com/spot/hatecrimes.html>.

Sider, G. 1987. When parrots learn to talk, and why they can't: Domination, deception, and self deception in indian-white relations. *Comparative Studies in Society and History, 20*(1), 3–23.

Simonsen, C., & Spindlove, J. 2000. *Terrorism Today: The Past, the Players, the Future*. Upper Saddle River, NJ: Prentice Hall.

Sims, P. 1996. *The Klan*. Lexington, KY: UP of Kentucky.

Smith v. Doe, 000 U.S. 01-729 (2003)

Southern Poverty Law Center (n.d.). A hundred years of terror. <http://www. iupui.edu/ ~aao/kkk.html>.

Sowell, T. 2002. *Beyond the Color Line: Discriminating, Economics, and Culture*. Boston, MA: Allyn and Bacon.

Sturdivant, D. 1994. *Youth Organizations: Gangs*. Unpublished Field Investigation Report. Compton, CA: July 8–12: 7–10.

Support for ICWA Amendments in S.1213, The National Congress of American Indians Res. PSC-99-034 (adopted Oct. 3–8, 1999). <http://130.94. 214.68/data/docs/ resolution/1999_annual_session/PSC99.034.htm>.

Takaki, R. 1989. *Strangers from a Different Shore: A History of Asian Americans*. Boston, MA: Little, Brown Publishers.

Takaki, R. 1993. *A Different Mirror: A History of Multicultural America*. Boston, MA: Little, Brown.

Taylor, R. Gottfredson, S., & Schumaker, S. 1984. *Neighborhood Response to Disorder*. Baltimore, MD: Center for Metropolitan Planning and Research, Johns Hopkins University.

Tessman, L. 1999. The radical politics of mixed race. *Journal of Social Philosophy, 30*(2), 276–294.

Thornton, R. 1998. *Studying Native America: Problems and Prospects*. Madison, WI: University of Wisconsin Press.

Thornton, R. 1987. *American Indian Holocaust and Survival*. Norman, OK: University of Oklahoma Press.

Title VII of the Civil Rights Act of 1964, 42 U.S.C. §2000e et seq.

Title XI of the Violent Crime Control and Law Enforcement Act of 1994 (Crime Control Act), Pub. L. No. 103-322, 108 Stat. 1796 (1994).

Todorov, T. 1993. *Human Diversity.* Cambridge, MA: Harvard University Press.

Tonry, M. 1995. *Malign Neglect: Race, Crime, and Punishment in America.* New York, NY: Oxford University Press.

28 U.S.C. § 1865(b) (1968). (Part V—Procedure, Chapter 121—Juries; Trial by Jury).

Uniting and Strengthening America by Providing Appropriate Tools Required to Intercept and Obstruct Terrorism (USA PATRIOT ACT) Act of 2001, Pub. L. No. 107-56, 115 Stat. 273 (signed into law Oct. 26, 2001).

University of California Regents v. Bakke, 438 U.S. 265 (1978)

U.S. Census Bureau, Population Division and Housing and Household Economic Statistics Division. 2001. National Population Projections. <http://www.census.gov/ population/www/pop-profile/natproj.html>.

U.S. Department of Justice, Federal Bureau of Investigation. 1993. *Crime in the United States, 1993.* Uniform Crime Reports. Washington, DC: Government Printing Office.

Van den Berghe, P. 1981. *The Ethnic Phenomenon.* New York, NY: Elsevier Publishers.

Vetter, H.J. & Perlstein, G.R. 1991. *Perspectives on Terrorism.* Belmont, CA: Wadsworth Publishing.

Virginia v. Black, 000 U.S. 01-1107 (2003)

Wallace, H. 1998. *Victimology: Legal, Psychological, and Social Perspectives.* Boston, MA: Allyn and Bacon.

Walker, S. 1977. *A Critical History of Police Reform.* Lexington, MA: Lexington Books.

Walker, S. 1981. *Police in America: An Introduction.* New York, NY: McGraw-Hill.

Walker, S. 1999. *Police in America: An Introduction* (3rd ed.). New York, NY: McGraw-Hill.

Walker, S., & Katz, C. 2002. *The Police in America.* New York, NY: McGraw-Hill.

Waters, K.L., Simoni, J.M., & Evans-Campbell, T. 2002. Substance use among american indians and alaska natives: Incorporating culture in an "indigenist" stress-coping paradigm. *Public Health Reports 2002,* 117 Suppl. 1, 104–117.

Weigel, G. 1994. *Idealism Without Illusions.* Grand Rapids, MI: William B. Eerdmans Publishing Company.

Weyr, T. 1988. *Hispanic U.S.A.* Philadelphia, PA: Harper & Rowe Publishers.

Whitcomb, D. 2004, January 26. Federal judge strikes down part of patriot act. *Reuters.* <http://foi.missouri.edu/usapatriotact/federaljudge.html>.

White, J. 2002. *Terrorism: An Introduction*. Belmont, CA: Wadsworth Thomson Learning.

White, J. 2004. *Defending the Homeland*. Belmont, CA: Wadsworth Thomson Learning.

Wilkinson, P. 1986. *Terrorism and the Liberal State*. New York, NY: New York University Press.

Wilkinson, P. 1993. *Technology and Terrorism*. Portland, OR: International Specialized Book Services, Inc.

Wilson, A. 1990. *Black-on-Black Violence*. New York, NY: Afrikan World Infosystems.

Wilson, J.Q. 1968. *Varieties of Police Behavior*. Cambridge, MA: Harvard University Press.

Wong, M.G. 1995. Chinese americans. In P.G. Min (Ed.), *Asian Americans: Contemporary Trends and Issues*. Thousand Oaks, CA: Sage Publications.

Wong, M.G. 2005. Chinese americans. In P.G. Min (Ed.), *Asian Americans: Contemporary Trends and Issues*. Thousand Oaks, CA: Sage Publications.

Worcester v. Georgia, 31 U.S. 515 (1832)

Worden, A. 1993. The attitudes of women and men in policing: Testing conventional and contemporary wisdom. *Criminology, 31*(2), 203–24.

Wu, J., & Song, M. 2000. *Asian American Studies*. Piscataway, NJ: Rutgers University Press.

Zogby, J. 2003. A national leadership conference that counts. <http://www.aaiusa.org/ wwatch/100603.htm>.

Zogby, J. 2002. *Healing the Nation: The Arab American Experience after September 11*. Washington, DC: Arab American Institute.

Index